Sweethearts WITH A MISSION

When You Serve with Love,
You Love to Serve

Sweethearts WITH A MISSION

When You Serve with Love, You Love to Serve

RANDY L. BOTT

CFI
An imprint of Cedar Fort, Inc.
Springville, Utah

ISBN 13: 978–1–4621–3937-8

Published by CFI, an imprint of Cedar Fort, Inc.
2373 W. 700 S., Springville, UT, 84663
Distributed by Cedar Fort, Inc., www.cedarfort.com

Library of Congress Control Number: 2021939731

Cover design by Courtney Proby

Printed in the United States of America

10 9 8 7 6 5 4 3 2 1

Printed on acid-free paper

CONTENTS

Sweethearts with a Mission

You're sweethearts with a mission.
You have a special work to do.
You're a treasure in God's service.
Because you're faithful, good and true.

Most missionaries stay arm's length
But you go hand in hand
Sharing a special message of
Your Father's eternal plan.

You're set apart together to build
And lift and teach.
But the example you show to others
Is the silent sermon that you preach.

You've learned to love each other
In a sacred, caring way.
You build and lift and harvest
By the things you do and say.

United, you serve together
Separate people bound as one.
You'll share sorrows, joy, and laughter
Until this work is done.

You'll share your dreams together
To build God's kingdom here on earth.
You've proved you are His children
Born of a noble birth.

And when you reach the other side
He'll say, "My dears, well done.
You were sweethearts with a mission
And now forever you'll be as one."

So hold your companion dearly
As you serve, and teach, and love.
You're building for eternity
Your mansion up above.

—Sister Vickie P. Bott

INTRODUCTION

A word of explanation might help you understand this book better. Over twenty-seven years ago my wife and I were released from a three-year calling as mission president. For the next two decades I taught missionary preparation at Brigham Young University in Provo, Utah, to thousands of preparing missionaries.

Because a formal curriculum was not available at the time, I was instructed to write my own. As I taught, I compiled three volumes: *Prepare with Honor, Serve with Honor,* and *Home with Honor,* which Deseret Book published and still sells twenty years later.

I realized that we had enjoyed a close association with senior missionary couples and had noted the incalculable contributions they made to the mission, as well as some of the challenges they faced. Being in the writing mode, I started this book aptly named by my wife: *Sweethearts with a Mission.*

For some reason I would write a few chapters, and then the developing manuscript would be shelved for some years. A talk or presentation by one of our leaders would jump-start my thinking again. I would write a few more chapters, and then the cycle repeated.

That is so unlike me that I wondered if I shouldn't write this book. Recently as I pondered my dilemma, I recalled two lectures I had attended some years before on marriage and parenting. The lecturer was a woman in her mid-fifties, professional, polished, entertaining, and very knowledgeable. The first lecture was on how to build a solid, enduring, and happy marriage. It was insightful and entertaining. I took copious notes. However, several of her suggestions seemed to run contrary to our experience.

The next lecture was on strategies for successfully raising children. When this lecture was given, we had four of our six children. Again, she had some very relevant and applicable insights, but several of her suggestions, although they sounded good, hadn't been successful in our parenting experience.

After the lectures were over, I more carefully read her bio. I discovered that she had never married but had chosen a professional career instead. Therefore, she did not have firsthand experience with marriage or raising children. Her expertise was gained through research and personal observation but not from personal experience. In no way would I demean the value of research and observation. It was great but incomplete. Sometimes the "book learning" sounded really good but just didn't work when tried in the crucible of personal experience.

In a heartbeat I realized that although I had served a full-time mission as a young man, had been a stake mission president twice, and had served as a mission president, I had only observed senior couple missionaries. It shouldn't have been a surprise to me that following our recently completed couple mission to Hawaii, I could now write from personal experiences coupled with the research and observation over the past twenty years.

So, twenty years after starting this book, the combined experience of working alongside more than one hundred couples at BYU—Hawaii, the visitors' center, the temple missionaries, and the wonderful PCC (Polynesian Culture Center) missionaries, I had a much better grasp of what couples actually experience.

After a year's rest following our mission to Hawaii, we decided to go once again since our health was good. We were called to the Sydney Australia Mission and served with some of the most wonderful, powerful missionaries and leaders on the face of the earth. It was so exhilarating that we submitted our papers again, hoping to return to Australia. However, the Covid-19 pandemic has put our calls on hold. Who knows how long the pause will last or if, by the time things settle down, we may be too old to serve. In either case, the need for senior missionaries has never been greater. Our vision of the impact senior missionaries have has broadened with every call. What a time to put in your papers for the greatest experience of your life as seniors.

Now I am faced with another dilemma. Do I go back and update the quotes from General Authorities, some of whom have passed away, or do I stick with those I gathered over the past twenty years? Since those of you who will be reading this book are likely more familiar with General Authorities of some years ago than those who are presently being called, I have decided to stick with the original quotes. In doing so I confess some of the most solicitous invitations to serve have been given by current leaders. I encourage all of you to search out the most recent quotes. They will only emphasize and underscore the critical need for more senior missionaries.

I dedicate this work to the thousands of senior couples who have stepped out of their comfort zone, responded to the prophet's call, and sacrificed their way into immortal glory.

Chapter 1

A CALL FROM THE LORD

Think of it. Of all the billions of people who have and now inhabit this globe, you are among the select few who have the opportunity to receive, through authorized servants, the mind and will of the Lord directly to you! Countless generations have been born, lived out their lives, and died without ever hearing the voice of a living prophet. You are among the chosen people who do not have to wonder if you are doing the Lord's will or guess if He is pleased with your choices. It is no wonder that Latter-day Saints all over the world join in joyous song, raising our voices heavenward with the strain "We thank thee O God for a prophet, to guide us in these latter-day. We thank thee for sending the gospel, to lighten our minds with its rays. We thank thee for every blessing bestowed by thy bounteous hand. We feel it a pleasure to serve thee and love to obey thy command" (Hymn no. 19).

For whatever part of your lives you have been members, you have responded to the life-saving counsel of the living prophets. Probably more than any other people on earth, you can stand as a witness that the Lord really has revealed the plan of happiness. You have lived long enough to discover first hand that "wickedness never was happiness" (Alma 41:10). There is so much sorrow and heartache in the world, much of which can be directly attributed to the breaking of God's commandments. You have long since discovered by observation (sometimes by sad experience) that which the younger generation seems destined to learn by painful suffering, that is, that there is no other way to peace and happiness outside the guidelines given to us by the Lord.

Now, standing as it were near the finish line of mortality, too many couples seem content to sit back and take a much needed and deserved breather. However, the Lord has something different in mind. He, through His living prophets, has issued the call to serve one more time. President Ezra Taft Benson said, "Now I want to say a few words to some of you older brethren. We have need for select missionary couples."[1] Perhaps President Benson addressed the men because we men need to be the ones who initiate the action. Four years later President Benson renewed the call to arms: "As a mature couple, having reared your children, have you prayerfully considered serving a full-time mission? The Lord needs many more couples in the mission field who can love and fellowship and lead people to Christ.[2]

The idea of senior couples serving missions is not new. Over sixty years ago, President Stephen L. Richards of the First Presidency said: "We have need for married couples in the missions—men and women of maturity and experience whose families have been reared, who can go into missions and not only proselyte but also teach to branches of the mission the great principles of self-government, to give guidance under the direction of the mission president to the efforts of new members who have not been schooled in the procedures of the Church."[3]

As the population of the Church continues to mature, it would seem that being a prophet-following people, we would have flooded the earth with seasoned, mature couples who are ready to step up to the plate and assume their God-given duties. However, in 1980, President Spencer W. Kimball pointed out that we were falling far short of our potential. He said: "Eight percent of the total missionary force is represented by older couples. What a blessing their maturity and experience are wherever they serve. With the divine commission we have to share the gospel with the entire world, we do indeed need many more missionaries. Remember that 'the field is white already to harvest' (D&C 4:4)."[4]

Echoing the words of President Kimball, Elder Jack H. Goaslind of the Seventy combined the call with an explanation of the benefit received by all who serve no matter what their age:

> Young men, do you understand why President Spencer W. Kimball said that "every young man should fill a mission?" (*Ensign*, Oct. 1974, p. 8.) It is not an option; it is your obligation to serve. And do you mature couples understand that President Kimball has made it clear that you also have this responsibility? (See *The Teachings of Spencer W. Kimball*, ed. Edward L. Kimball, Salt Lake City: Bookcraft, 1982, p. 551.) He said, "The time is at hand to go." (Go Ye into All the World, text from a film produced by Brigham Young University Department of Motion Picture Production, Provo: Brigham Young University, 1974, p. 2.) This service is as much for your benefit as it is for the benefit of the Church and the nonmembers who receive your message. We are grateful for the increasing numbers of young men and couples who are serving missions. We assure you that there is no more important thing you can do than prepare for a mission by prayerfully studying the scriptures, keeping yourselves morally clean, and conducting your temporal and spiritual lives with the goal of a mission firmly in mind.[5]

Being numbered himself among the senior Saints, Elder David B. Haight talked of the "distinguishing features of wrinkles and graying hair" as he renewed the call for more older couples to serve. "There are many hundreds of experienced, devoted couples—those whose hair may be graying and perhaps with a wrinkle here or there—you know, those distinguishing features of maturity—that are retiring from their professional careers but with several productive years still remaining before their golden years, whose children have made lives of their own, who are in good health, and who dream of that eventful moment when they say to their bishop, 'We're ready—ready to do something really important—to go on a mission, to go anywhere the Lord needs us.'"[6]

Some couples may be holding back because their overworked bishop hasn't issued them a challenge to go. Don't be shy! Do as Elder Haight suggested and tell your bishop you are ready to serve. President Gordon B. Hinckley further urged the bishops: "Bishops can and should appraise the older couples in their wards who might be eligible for missionary service and who can give needed service under some circumstances."[7] Every day you wait for someone to recognize your abilities and willingness to serve is one more day you are not out in the field doing the most rewarding work in the world—saving the souls of your brothers and sisters.

You may be worried about not being qualified. Although a later chapter will be devoted to that very topic, it would be well to re-read what President James E. Faust said a number of years ago: "Bishops or stake presidents should have qualified couples or single sisters attach to their regular missionary application a brief outline of their education, their work experience, and their hobbies or other talents. You should know that there is currently a need for couples with ability in languages other than English. At present, the greatest needs are for Spanish speakers."[8] Not only can you perform an invaluable service in teaching the gospel, but even your hobbies and talents can enrich the lives of those you serve. No matter what your educational level is, no matter how you earned your living during your working years, no matter what perceived limitations you have, no matter what spiritual or scriptural deficiencies you think you have, you are needed in the growing army of missionaries in the latter days. Remember President Monson's oft quoted statement: "Whom God calls God qualifies."

Is it a scary thing? Probably! Almost everything we undertake that is new and untried can cause some fear. However, remember the word of the Lord through the Apostle Paul to his son in the faith, Timothy: "For God has not given us the spirit of fear, but of power, and of love, and of a sound mind" (2 Timothy 1:7). If that fear doesn't come from the Lord, where does it come from? You're right! From the adversary. Since his stated objective is to make us miserable like unto himself (see 2 Nephi 2:18, 27), and since we are informed that he "is a liar from the very beginning" (see D&C 93:25), why should we listen to his lies that we are not good enough, not healthy enough, not smart enough, not financially well off enough, not spiritual enough to serve a mission?

The Lord outlined the prerequisites for joining His army of missionaries: "Therefore, if ye have desires to serve God ye are called to the work" (D&C 4:3). Why not talk it over this very day? Talk with other couples who have served. You will find an almost universal response that the mission was the greatest thing they have ever done as a couple. It is not difficult for us to envision a reunion in the paradise of God. Those present may well include the couples who have valiantly served throughout the world, the eternally grateful converts who owe not only their eternal life but also their mortal happiness to the missionaries, and the Perfect One who gave His life to bless us all. In fact, the Lord suggested such a reunion. In Doctrine and Covenants 18:14–16, He said: "Wherefore, you are called to cry repentance unto this people. And if it so be that you should labor all your days in crying repentance unto this people, and bring, save it be one soul unto me, how great shall be your joy with him in the kingdom of my Father! And now, if your joy will be great with one soul that you have brought unto me into the kingdom of my Father, how great will be your joy if you should bring many souls unto me!"

In the chapters that follow, our intent is to address, in a very practical way, some of the questions and concerns that couples have when considering a mission. Although selected quotes from the Brethren will be used and a limited number of scriptures cited, the majority of this work will be based on the experience my wife and I enjoyed as mission president as we interfaced with the senior couples in our mission and our most recent experiences as we served as senior missionaries at BYU—Hawaii and in Sydney, Australia. We shared countless hours with them in serious doctrinal discussions, in fun-filled dinners, in Spirit-directed zone conferences, and in personal interviews. Truthfully, we learned more from them than they learned from us. The friendships we fostered while engaged in a common cause has made us many lifelong friends. Perhaps we error in saying "lifelong friends," for some of our beloved missionaries have since departed to the next life. More appropriately we should say we have made many wonderful "eternal friends."

To those couples who demonstrated by their daily acts of kindness and service, who gave a full measure in the work of the Lord, who served without complaint under trying conditions, we dedicate this work. Thanks be to God for being privileged to participate in this latter-day miracle of senior couple missionaries.

NOTES

1. Ezra Taft Benson, *Ensign*, May 1984, 45.
2. Ibid., *Ensign*, May 1988, 84.
3. Stephen L. Richards, in Conference Report, October 1955, 98.
4. Spencer W. Kimball, *Ensign*, May 1980, 4.
5. Jack H. Goaslind, *Ensign*, November 1983, 34.
6. David B. Haight, *Ensign*, May 1987, 60.
7. Gordon B. Hinckley, in Conference Report, October 1965, 102.
8. James E. Faust, "Establishing the Church: Welfare Services Missionaries Are an Important Resource," *Ensign*, November 1979, 92.

Chapter 2

CAN WE TOLERATE EACH OTHER FOR A YEAR OR MORE?

Although some may be inclined to laugh at the title of this chapter, we have discovered in talking with numerous couples that it is a very real concern. After all, for most, if not all, of your married lives you have lived under the same roof but had very different roles. If you come from the traditional mode, the husband has been off earning a living while the wife has been at home bearing and rearing the children and tending to the home. Although you may have spent many wonderful times together in the evenings, on weekends, and on vacations, the majority of your twenty-four-hour day was spent either sleeping or working.

For many couples the transition into retirement presents some unique challenges. What does the wife do with her husband underfoot all day long? Occasionally tempers flare and harsh words are exchanged. Although not as prevalent among Latter-day Saints, the number of couples divorcing after retirement is rising at an alarming rate. Far too many people discover after retirement that they are two strangers living under the same roof. Wouldn't it be a mistake to take those problems into the mission field? The answer would be a resounding "yes" if you were just going to continue your lives as at present but in the mission field.

The fact is that your entire focus of your lives will change when you accept a mission call. Whereas one of the major problems plaguing retired couples is that they are living two separate and distinct lives, in the mission field you are both immersed in a common cause. Your lives become so intertwined that you learn to always say "we" and "us" rather than "I" and "mine." Whereas your focus during retirement is almost entirely on yourselves, in the mission you hardly have the time to consider your own needs because of the pressing needs you are meeting for other people. Whereas in retirement you have many leisure hours when demands are not made on your time, in the mission there is always much more to do than you have time and energy to accomplish. This list goes on and on. The life you are living now hardly resembles the life you will be living in the mission field.

For many years now, you have been meeting the challenges of life together. Although blessed with the gifts of the gospel and busied with family and church work, it seems that many of the difficult decisions had to be worked out between you and your children. There may have been some very rough times and even some major disagreements. But you survived. In the mission field you will also be faced with some very difficult problems, but because you are on the Lord's errand, He (under the hands of the stake president) gives you a special mantle before you go. What is the mantle? Consider who you represent and you'll discover the answer. In 1 John 4:16, John explains: "And we have known and believed the love that God hath to us. God is love; and he that dwelleth in love dwelleth in God, and God in him." Because "God is love" and you represent God, the mantle that covers both of you is one of love.

Almost without exception, the couples we worked with said that the mission was the greatest unifier they had ever experienced in their married lives. Elder L. Tom Perry, quoting a senior missionary couple he had interviewed, said: "The privilege of serving a full-time mission together was an outstanding time in our lives. It was a time during which we drew close together as we studied and prayed so much together. We learned more fully to depend upon one another. We found great joy in becoming more aware of one another's strengths. We anticipated the opportunity of helping each other overcome our weaknesses. In the autumn of our lives, it was a time of ripening and cementing together. This is an experience every couple should have if they are physically able and can financially afford it."[1]

Even if you have been diligent as a family in reading scriptures and saying family prayers, you will find the frequency and intensity with which you engage in these sacred rites is greatly increased during your missions. Sometimes we found that couples had spent so much time teaching and training their children that they had neglected their own individual and couple needs in order to provide for the children. Now is a golden time to rectify that mistake. Wives confided in us that they had no idea of the depth of their husband's understanding and testimony of the gospel. Many couples reported that they had never enjoyed family home evening so much as they did while serving missions. Many husbands marveled at the depth of wisdom and comprehension their wives had of gospel principles. Some said they had never heard their spouse bear such a fervent testimony of the gospel before their missions.

While it is also true that differences were identified, under the influence of the mantle of love, almost all couples reported that they were more patient, more forgiving, more understanding of each other as they worked together to overcome lifelong weaknesses. When we probed deeper to determine why the increased patience, many concluded that they did not want to do anything that could possibly detract from the Spirit in their teaching. Therefore, they were more highly motivated to solve their differences in a way that did not drive the Spirit away. After a number of months of solving differences, we began to notice almost a "glow" come from the couples. Our conclusion was that as they became one with each other as the Father and the Son are one, that the love of the Father dwelt in them more abundantly. The whole chapter of 1 John 4 bears re-reading as a couple to see what the Lord has promised those who love each other.

It seems to have been far too easy to have ignored differences during the former years of marriage. However, ignored weaknesses are still weaknesses. Joseph Smith gave us a vision and a challenge in a single statement: "If you wish to go where God is, you must be like God, or possess the principles which God possesses; for if we are not drawing towards God in principles, we are going from Him and drawing towards the devil. Yes, I am standing in the midst of all kinds of people. Search your hearts, and see if you are like God. I have searched mine, and feel to repent of all my sins."[2]

Nowhere that we know about is the desire to identify and overcome weaknesses as strong as in the mission field. We have witnessed tremendous growth in both husbands and wives as they address their weaknesses together, and, strengthened by the help of the Almighty, they have successfully overcome irritating habits, obnoxious traits, and perceived weaknesses that have plagued them for years. They have returned home (sometimes to the amazement of their children) more like honeymooners than old married fogies.

Many of our senior couples confided that it was in the watching their mate teach the gospel to and work with the people that they discovered a new side that they had not noticed before. Even as a mission president, I gained a much greater appreciation for my wife and her multi-dimensional talents than I ever had before the mission. Many couples discovered in the mission field how truly smart they had been years before when they chose their eternal companion. The true depth of a person's soul is more clearly seen as they wrestle in the Spirit to bring souls unto Christ. The vision of the eternal possibilities of each individual seem to be more evident as we serve missions than at any other time.

In all honesty, there were couples who struggled to get along until they forgot themselves into immortal glory. It was just as apparent with the couples as it was when the young missionaries got their own testimony. When the couples became one, their entire countenance changed. There was more tenderness between them. There was more willingness to communicate and solve problems. There was more concern for the companion spouse than for themselves. There was more of an "eternal world" perceptive than we had noticed before. They seemed to enjoy each other more and have more fun together than before they received that "born again together" type of experience.

One of the statements that put missions into perspective more for us than almost any other was made by our Area Presidency. They said that the General Authorities had calculated that a two-year mission was equivalent to fifty years of normal Church service. Think of that! If you serve for a year, you have just logged the equivalent of twenty-five years of experience. An eighteen-month mission would calculate to thirty-seven and a half years of church experience. Since there are two of you serving, you have just accumulated seventy-five years' worth of church experience, credit, and rewards for your service! You can't beat those returns anywhere.

Included in that service is the knowledge you receive and the power that is given to both of you to live more Christlike lives. The Lord never gives us an assignment without providing ways and means to accomplish the required task (see 1 Nephi 3:7). Why not put the Lord to the test? See if the mission doesn't do for you what you had dreamed you would be like before you ever got married.

You might ask, "We have a very good relationship already. Why should we serve?" There are three very good reasons: (1) the Lord has asked you to serve; (2) your relationship will still soar to even greater heights than you dreamed possible; and (3) you will bless the lives of countless other people (including other senior couples) who need a role model in order to know how to "celestialize" their relationship.

Obviously, the more stable your relationship before you go into the mission field, the more progress you can make in doing the Lord's work. But the fear of not being able to get along well enough to succeed is yet another false tactic of the adversary in his devilish attempt to stop you from serving. It would be good advice for all of us to sit down frequently and identify the possible areas where the adversary could penetrate our armor and cause dissension between us. Then go to with your might and eliminate the chinks in your armor. By seriously addressing the areas of potential conflict, you will discover that you are more resilient than you thought. The least little difference will not be marriage threatening.

Before ending this chapter, let us consider another group who make great missionaries. We refer to those who have recently lost their mates and have just found someone else they can love and enjoy for the rest of their mortal lives. We are talking about the "senior newlyweds." It was always amusing and thrilling to have a newly wedded senior couple come to the mission field. Of course, they needed to be prepared for some good-natured ribbing—not only from the other couples but also from the young missionaries, and possibly even the mission president and his wife. They were not trying to be cruel, but were thrilled at the couple's willingness to embark on an eighteen-month honeymoon to begin their life together.

These precious couples seemed to breathe life into all of our marriages. They were so much in love and so desirous to serve each other that it gave us "old marrieds" somewhat of a jump-start. We were not about to be out done by these newlyweds! Several of these couples reported that there was some resistance to their proposed marriages from both families. When it became clear that Dad wanted to serve a mission and couldn't unless he had a wife, much of the resistance disappeared. The children seemed to see that their resistance was really the result of selfishness. No one was going to replace Mom. Even the new wife did not cause Dad to forget either Mom or the kids. In every case we were privileged to observe the second marriage that had its beginnings in the mission field, the mission field was the method of erasing any walls of resistance in having each partner accepted into the respective families.

We witnessed miracles as the families would come to visit their "honeymooning" parents and see the joy they were experiencing together and the good they were doing. The families would leave with an added sense of appreciation for the selfless work their parents were engaged in.

We have an abiding testimony that missions cement relationships. We do not hesitate to promise that the Lord will fulfill the promise He made to those who are diligent and faithful in his service:

> For thus saith the Lord—I, the Lord, am merciful and gracious unto those who fear me, and delight to honor those who serve me in righteousness and in truth unto the end. Great shall be their reward and eternal shall be their glory. And to them will I reveal all mysteries, yea, all the hidden mysteries of my kingdom from days of old, and for ages to come, will I make known unto them the good pleasure of my will concerning all things pertaining to my kingdom. Yea, even the wonders of eternity shall they know, and things to come will I show them, even the things of many generations. And their wisdom shall be great, and

> their understanding reach to heaven; and before them the wisdom of the wise shall perish, and the understanding of the prudent shall come to naught. For by my Spirit will I enlighten them, and by my power will I make known unto them the secrets of my will—yea, even those things which eye has not seen, nor ear heard, nor yet entered into the heart of man. (D&C 76:5–10)

So, if one of the mysteries happens to be how to get along with each other, why not put the Lord to the test and see if He isn't willing to reveal even that mystery unto you? It has worked wondrously well in our own lives. It worked miraculously well in the lives of our senior couples. We are convinced that it will work equally as well in your own lives. Don't pass up the greatest experience of your married lives because of an ungrounded fear. Sign up now and watch the miracle happen in your own lives.

NOTES

1. L. Tom Perry, *Ensign*, May 1984, 80.
2. *Teachings of the Prophet Joseph Smith*, 216.

Chapter 3

HOW CAN WE LEAVE THE CHILDREN AND GRANDCHILDREN?

As reported by our senior missionaries and confirmed by our own experience, by far the most difficult obstacle couples face in deciding to serve a mission is the challenge to leave family. Often it is not the children who pose the greatest challenge, but the grandchildren! Many of them are very young and changing so rapidly it is difficult to envision not being there to enjoy their growing up. We wish there was a way of making the parting with family less painful, but it is a decision that will have to be made by each couple.

Because missions for couples are of varying length, it may not become so critical an issue. Although not recommended, the Church will permit six-month missions for couples. From our experience, one possible reason they do not encourage six-month missions is it takes some time to get into the routine of missionary work. About the time you become really effective, your six months is over and you're heading home. A second reason may be that it costs just as much to travel to and from the mission field whether you stay for six, twelve, or eighteen months. In order to maximize your (and the Church's) investment, going from twelve to eighteen months is much more desirable. Elder A. Theodore Tuttle said:

> The nature of your service will not be exactly like the young missionaries. The emphasis now is for experienced couples to teach leadership principles (which you already know) to inexperienced leaders. Normally you will not preside in a branch or district, but you will help those who do to improve their abilities and to cause the Church to function properly. You will also teach principles of personal and family preparedness. You might work as a specialist in health, agriculture or vocational services. You will share the gospel through proselyting as well. The length of service is usually eighteen months. However, you may serve a six- or twelve-month mission.[1]

Our experience was that couples who stayed for one year were very effective and comfortable with that length of service. It was not unusual for a couple to "re-up" for an additional six months or a year beyond the length of their original call.

How can you minimize the impact on your family by your leaving? Just leave! When your enthusiasm for the service is communicated to your family, they will see that this mission is something that you really want to do. They will not want to stand in the way of your service. If you look at your mission as being a burdensome drudgery, you will also communicate that spirit to your family.

Elder Dallin H. Oaks shares the enthusiasm of what multiple missions do for senior couples. "Time after time, the pioneers President Clark praised left their homes, loaded their wagons, and moved to new hardships at the direction of their prophet. In our day, many couples go on mission after mission. One dear veteran described her family's reaction: 'Our children say, We hope you'll come by and at least have dinner with us before you go on another mission.'"[2]

We can still hear the threatening warning of a family whose parents had extended for six months as they jokingly told us not to encourage them to extend again. We can also remember vividly the parents calling after being home for a month and wondering if they should come back and serve again. They did return and went for yet another six months.

How can you stand to be parted for so long from your family? It isn't like you will be totally isolated from them. President Ezra Taft Benson added some helpful insight into this problem:

> Grandparents can have a profound influence on their grandchildren. Their time is generally not as encumbered and busy as the parents', so books can be opened and read, stories can be told, and application of gospel principles taught. Children then obtain a perspective of life which is not only rewarding but can bring them security, peace, and strength. It is possible to send letters, tapes, and pictures, particularly where distances are great and it is not possible to see one another often. Those who are blessed with a closeness to grandparents and other elderly people have a rich companionship and association. There might be times when they can attend graduations, weddings, temple excursions, missionary farewells and homecomings, and other special events with family members.[3]

Letters, emails, videos, pictures, Facetime, and Skype sessions often have a profound influence on children and grandchildren. Something about the letters written from the mission field have more powerful and lasting impact on the readers than just normal letters. Encouragement to children and grandchildren of a more spiritual nature is almost expected because you are serving a mission.

With the advent of the internet and Facebook, Twitter, Skype, and a host of other modern discoveries, there is no need for grandparents to be separated from their family. The restrictions that apply to young missionaries on communicating with loved ones at home do not apply to senior missionaries. In some cases, seniors are permitted to return home for special events and then return to their missionary service.

There is yet another positive influence that your serving a mission will have on your posterity. Elder Vaughan J. Featherstone said: "Thousands of mature couples and widowed missionaries could be called if they would simply make themselves available. Many of us understand the blessings that come when children and grandchildren kneel down at night and say, 'Dear Heavenly Father, please bless grandma and grandpa who are out in Texas on a mission.'"[4]

Depending on where you serve, family visits to the mission field are not out of the question. With the permission of your mission president, families are often encouraged to make short visits to you in the mission field. Understanding that missionary apartments are modest and small, you might ask, how could our family come visit us? One of our senior couples had family come for a few days. They all brought sleeping bags and stayed on the floor in the combined living room/kitchen area. The grandchildren thought that was really fun. Even the children didn't mind sleeping on a couch for a couple of nights. They all thought it was like camping. The spirit of the grandparents completely erased any feelings of pity the children may have had.

Another couple celebrated their fiftieth anniversary in the field. They worried about accommodations since housing in a motel would be expensive for their families. One of the local families who worked with the couples learned of their plight. Not willing to take no for an answer, they informed the couple that they were going out of town for a week and wanted them to use their spacious six-bedroom home for their family. The children and grandchildren thought that Grandma and Grandpa had died and gone to heaven when they saw the home with a large swimming pool, tennis courts, and a trampoline. For the few days they spent there working with their grandparents in doing missionary work, much good was done. Upon their departure, one young granddaughter said she didn't want to leave. She wanted to stay forever with Grandma and Grandpa in their "missionary apartment" and be a missionary just like her grandparents.

Senior couples are not under the same restrictions as young missionaries about calling home. In fact, we encouraged our senior couples to talk with their families as frequently as necessary to fulfill their parental responsibility. Using the internet and other programs, the expense of long-distance calling is eliminated. Many seniors kept their local cell phone numbers so that calls were not billed as long distance no matter where they served. On our most recent mission (Sydney, Australia) we were able to call Sister Bott's sister and her husband, who were serving a temple mission in South Africa. Since we live about five miles apart in Utah, there were no long-distance charges from their cell phone to ours.

From our own and the experience of every couple we worked with and have talked to, it is universally agreed that the time they spent away from their families had a very positive influence on everyone. Even when children were not enthusiastically involved in the

Church, they were very supportive of their parents serving a mission. Many of the children who were struggling with being fully active caught the spirit and either worked themselves into full activity or were working their way back as their parents served.

The Lord knew exactly what impact the mission would have on children. In the early days of the Church in this dispensation, the Lord told Thomas B. Marsh: "Behold, you have had many afflictions because of your family; nevertheless, I will bless you and your family, yea, your little ones; and the day cometh that they will believe and know the truth and be one with you in my church. . . . Therefore, thrust in your sickle with all your soul, and your sins are forgiven you, and you shall be laden with sheaves upon your back, for the laborer is worthy of his hire. Wherefore, your family shall live" (D&C 31:2, 5).

We are not in a position to strengthen your family because of your missionary service—but the Lord is! You may have said that you need to stay home and strengthen your family before you embark in the service of the Lord. He promises that He will take care of your families if you do what He asks.

When Joseph Smith and Sidney Rigdon were away serving a mission in Canada and were concerned about the welfare of their families, the Lord revealed: "Verily, thus saith the Lord unto you, my friends Sidney and Joseph, your families are well; they are in mine hands, and I will do with them as seemeth me good; for in me there is all power. Therefore, follow me, and listen to the counsel which I shall give unto you" (D&C 100:1–2).

What a demonstration of faith in Him and His promise! Again, from our own personal experience and the experience of the couples we served with, our families were blessed far more by our being in the mission field than they would have been if we had stayed home. Some of those blessings are difficult to realize in the short term. But the promise of the Lord is sure: "Your family shall live" (D&C 31:5).

One senior couple made an unusual request. They wanted to leave the mission field long enough to re-baptize a daughter who had fallen away years before and been excommunicated. With the permission of the Area Presidency, approval was given. The spirit they brought back following the baptismal service infected the entire mission. The Lord really does follow through on His promises.

Brother Graham W. Doxey wrote an article for the *Ensign* concerning senior couples. He said:

> Pray to know God's will, not to "get things." Too often, because of our selfish desires, after a cursory "Thank you, Lord," we consume our prayer time in the listing of things we want, even of things we think we need. We must be willing to release the death grip which we have on things, which have become as a security blanket in our lives. Count the many hundreds of needed missionary couples who would be serving in the field if that firm grip on the familiarities of home and of children and grandchildren could be loosened. The Lord is prepared to perform the miracle that will follow, which miracle is that both they and you will survive, even grow, with an eighteen-month separation. We must learn to pray with meaning, "Not my will, but Thy will be done." When you are able to do this, his whisperings to you will be loud and clear. The Prophet Joseph Smith, after five months of extreme suffering in the dungeon of Liberty Jail, experienced it, and he said, "When the heart is sufficiently contrite, then the voice of inspiration steals along and whispers, My son, peace be unto thy soul."[5]

Are we willing to place enough trust in our Heavenly Father to let go of the things and even the people who have become so dear to us? This mission may constitute for you what the Lord said was necessary in order to complete the sanctification process in your lives. He said: "Therefore, they must needs be chastened and tried, even as Abraham, who was commanded to offer up his only son. For all those who will not endure chastening, but deny me, cannot be sanctified" (D&C 101:4–5).

We likely will not be asked to offer our children or grandchildren as human sacrifices, but we may be asked to "give them up" for a short year or year and a half. By being willing to offer Isaac as a sacrifice, Abraham gained for himself the promise of eternal posterity, which would be numberless as the stars in the heavens and the sands on the seashores. We can do the same by willingly sacrificing the pleasures of family associations for a short time with the promise of eternal associations in the life to come. The sacrifice hardly seems to merit the promised blessings.

Some may be concerned that their absence from their families would result in the break-up of the families. It would be well to remember as previously cited the promise the Lord gave to Joseph Smith and Sidney Rigdon when they were concerned about their families, having be absent from them for a long time: "Verily, thus saith the Lord unto you, my friends Sidney and Joseph, your families are well; they are in mine hands, and I will do with them as seemeth me good; for in me there is all power" (D&C 100:1).

Leave your families in the hands of the Lord. He has sufficient power and knowledge to do a far better job with them than we can. When you respond to the invitation to serve, the Lord offers to replace you as the stabilizing influence in the lives of your family. That is really where they should be looking for their strength and guidance anyway. Although we do not like to think about it, the day will come when we will not be present with our families. If their total stability in the Church and in their families has been dependent upon us, they will be in serious trouble. Won't you be doing your children a real service by gently forcing their dependence to shift from you to the Lord?

Can you leave your family? Yes, because the rewards both in time and in eternity will eclipse the sacrifice. You will not have to wait until the next life to see that what you have done for your family is the best sacrifice you could possibly make for them.

NOTES

1. A. Theodore Tuttle, *Ensign*, November 1977, 55–56.
2. Dallin H. Oaks, *Ensign*, November 1989, 65.
3. Ezra Taft Benson, *Ensign*, November 1989, 7.
4. Vaughn J. Featherstone, *Ensign*, November 1978, 26.
5. *History of the Church*, 3:293; Graham W. Doxey, *Ensign*, November 1991, 26.

Chapter 4

HOW MUCH WILL A MISSION COST?

Some missions are expensive. Some missions are very reasonable. Some missions are considerably less expensive than the day-to-day living you have experienced to this point in your lives. A lot depends on where you are assigned to serve your mission. The Church helps senior missionaries meet the costs. Housing and utilities have a monthly cap of $1400 (at the present time). The Church pays anything more than that.

An automatic withdrawal is taken from your ward account and funneled to Church headquarters. The difference in costs (for senior couples) is the food, travel within the mission field, and any other living expenses—there is a great variety depending on where you serve. You might want to check out ChurchofJesusChrist.org and look under Senior Missionaries for approximated costs in the different areas of the world. The costs of the missions (above and beyond housing and utilities) range from a hundred dollars a month to several hundreds dollars per month.

The Church will pay for mileage, motels, and meals when a couple's mission assignment is within the United States and Canada. Couples will be required to take their own car. If traveling to their assigned mission outside the United States or Canada, the Church pays for all travel expenses (air and ground transportation once arriving in the assigned country).

Couples are expected to finance their own expenses beyond the housing and utility payment. Generally, depending on where you serve, a mission car will be provided with a minimal monthly cost. What does that mean for different missions in dollars and cents? It would be impossible to attach an exact dollar amount because of the tremendous variations throughout the world. Even within the same mission field the expenses vary from couple to couple. For those couples where finances were not a serious issue, they would spend more than others who were required to watch their resources closely. You might be saying to yourselves, "Why, that is just a description of the way life is at home!" You are exactly right. In this regard, life in the mission field is no different from life at home. Some couples eat out on a regular basis. Others seldom frequent costly restaurants.

At the time you receive your mission call and assignment, you will receive communication from the mission president detailing the monthly costs as well as what items to take with you. Most of you will be pleasantly surprised that the suggested amount is very reasonable and well within your budget. For those who need to sit down and catch your breath when you see the monthly requirement, don't despair. By using a little creativity and a lot of inspiration (which the Lord promised He would give you), you will find that even the more expensive missions are very doable.

Let's consider some points to help allay any fears you may have about not being able to sustain yourselves financially in the mission field. To begin with, you are spending a certain amount of money right now just to stay alive. Whatever that amount is can automatically be transferred to offset your mission expense. In many places in the world, it is no more expensive to buy food and the basic necessities than it is at home. You are probably accustomed to cooking your own meals now. Doing the same thing in the mission field will not be burdensome. Our young missionaries loved to eat with the couples because they missed "Mom's cooking." Many young missionaries will offer to provide the food for the meal if the senior sister will cook it. They used to say: "It just doesn't taste the same when we cook as when Sister Jones does." Obviously, you will have to be reasonable about how frequently you cook for the young elders and sisters.

Many of you have been saving all of your lives for a rainy day. Well, at least part of that nest egg can be used for this sunny day experience. Many of you have been helping your children get started for many years. Not a few couples have been deeply touched when their children have come to them after holding a family meeting and informed them that they (the children) wanted to finance the mission for their parents. What a wonderful way of making them part of your mission. Grandchildren have contributed part of the money they earned from paper routes and other jobs. As you come to realize that missions bless everyone they touch, you will see that what you thought was a sacrifice for your children and grandchildren, in reality, is a tremendous blessing. Don't deprive them of the blessings because of a false sense of pride. Let them enjoy the unparalleled blessings of your mission with you (see Mark 9:41).

There are also many people in your ward and/or of your acquaintances whose health or present employment situation do not permit them to serve missions, but who would gladly help defray part of the monthly cost. One announcement in Relief Society meeting and elder's quorum meeting by the bishop could eliminate any financial concerns you may have. Again, it is not a matter of begging but an opportunity for those who cannot serve at present to do something that will greatly enrich their lives. You may have been in meetings over the years when requests have been made for help. Did you view that as begging? Neither will they.

You may also have members of your enlarged families who have been blessed financially by the Lord. Before you count them out as a possible source of income, make a contact with them. The enthusiasm you will exude about your call will be very infectious. Even if they have traditionally been sort of tight with their funds, you may see an entirely different side of them. You may also have friends who are available to help even though they are not in the "rich" group. Don't deprive them of the opportunity to sacrifice a little and receive the promised reward. Remember the words of the Savior: "He that receiveth you receiveth me, and he that receiveth me receiveth him that sent me. He that receiveth a prophet in the name of a prophet shall receive a prophet's reward; and he that receiveth a righteous man in the name of a righteous man shall receive a righteous man's reward. And whosoever shall give to drink unto one of these little ones a cup of cold water only in the name of a disciple, verily I say unto you, he shall in no wise lose his reward" (Matthew 10:40–42).

There are many other ways of eliminating the fear of not being able to afford a mission. When we returned from our service as mission president, we rented a home while we found a place to build. We only had access to three-fourths of the house because two large areas had been sealed off. When we asked about it, we discovered that the couple who owned the house was serving a mission in Southern California. All of their furniture and household items were stored in those two large rooms. The rent we paid monthly for the privilege of living in their home would have paid for their entire mission. In addition to paying the rent, there was a special spirit in the home that motivated us not only to take good care of it but to paint the trim on the outside of the house and make several minor repairs at our own expense because we knew what they were doing. Although we may have been unique because of our mission service, we were probably more typical than you would imagine. The Lord really does take care of His own.

When we left for our three-year mission, we rented our home to a relative of my wife's. She took care of the house and the yard as well or better than we did. Our house payment was adequately met by the rent, thus freeing us of any worry about finances. We were witnesses to the blessings of the Lord to virtually every couple who served with us.

If you have decided you don't want someone else living in your home and you have children or grandchildren living nearby who will take care of the upkeep for you, then you may still have resources available. Those of us who are old enough to retire lived during an era when large lots were the norm. As we age, the enthusiasm for gardening may still be there, but the physical ability to keep up is diminished. Have you considered selling a building lot from part of your farm or large city lot? The factor that may surprise you more than anything is what people are willing to pay for a lot. You may have purchased the entire farm or lot for a few hundred or thousand dollars. People often are willing to pay more for a postage stamp-sized building lot than you paid for the entire parcel. Are you being unfair by charging so much? Not at all! Find out what the going rate is for building lots, hire a land surveyor to mark off the lot, and prepare a description. Then see what the market will bear. You may be shocked to see that one building lot brings in sufficient money to finance several missions.

What if your lot is not large enough to subdivide or is located in an area where the prices have not gone through the ceiling? If you have lived in your home long enough, it is probably paid for. You are sitting on a gold mine. Although you would have to proceed with caution, and with the advice of a trusted financial counselor friend, you might consider a reverse mortgage. You keep the title to your home. You do not have to repay the money you withdraw, but you have use of the equity you have in your home. Again, there is a surprise factor. You may have purchased your home fifty years ago for fifty thousand dollars. Now you have it appraised for a reverse mortgage and discover that it is worth several hundred thousand dollars.

The obvious caution is that your home will not be free and clear when you pass away and the children sell the home. The advantage is that before they divide the proceeds from your home, all they will need to do is take the first part of the money and pay off the reverse mortgage before they divide the remainder. This may be a method of financing your mission and your retirement that you haven't considered yet. Again, proceed with caution and make sure you understand the entire process before you jump into something that you do not fully understand and will be a source of regret to you later on. Several of our couples were using the equity in their homes as the little "extra" they felt they needed to live comfortably in the mission field.

For those who are retired, Social Security checks come monthly no matter where you live. Many of you will have retirement accounts that also pay monthly just as easily in South Africa as they do at your home address. Pension plans pay out as need arise. Many of you may have money in CDs or money market accounts. Others may have invested in the stock market and are now ready to enjoy some of the rewards for their investments. Still others may have livestock they are worried about while they are gone. They may be sold for some handsome returns if liquid cash is a problem. Then you don't have to worry about someone taking care of them, and you can also enjoy the financial gains from their sale.

There is yet another source of income that many fail to consider. As young married couples you may have purchased furniture, bedroom sets, kitchen furniture, and so on, which you have replaced over the years with newer, more modern furniture. Rather than just throw the old stuff away, many couples stored it in the shed or in the basement. A few months ago we had a real revelation. We were on a speaking assignment in Texas and went to an antique mall. It was a huge building that was filled with "worthless old stuff." The revelation was that it wasn't "worthless old stuff" at all. The price tags on many of the items caused me to look for a chair to sit on and catch my breath. I couldn't sit down, however, because the chair I wanted to sit on was more expensive than our budget could afford. Do you have "old, worthless stuff" (antiques) stored away? Have someone who knows the market come over and appraise them. You might also receive a revelation when they disclose how much the items are worth.

You might be doing yourselves a double favor. How many times have you talked about cleaning out all that old stuff and taking it to DI but never got around to it? Cleaning out is even more fun when you see the inflated price people are willing to pay for your antiques. A pre-mission garage sale could be the icing on your mission cake. The second blessing is the financial freedom you receive from the sale of these antiques. Before you dismiss this suggestion as not applicable, take a walk through your basement or shed (probably both!) and solicit the help of a professional in assessing value.

From what we have discussed in this chapter, it should be evident that money is available to whomever is willing to serve. The Lord may inspire you to find other ways not mentioned here that will be even more lucrative for you. Would it be too bold to say that no one should use finances as an excuse for not serving? Let the Lord fulfill His challenging promise to "prove me now herewith, saith the Lord of hosts, if I will not open you the windows of heaven, and pour you out a blessing, that there shall not be room enough to receive it. And I will rebuke the devourer for your sakes, and he shall not destroy the fruits of your ground; neither shall your vine cast her fruit before the time in the field, saith the LORD of hosts. And all nations shall call you blessed: for ye shall be a delightsome land, saith the LORD of hosts" (Malachi 3:10–12).

If we sound a little too positive about your being able to financially afford your mission, it is because we have been witnesses time and time again to the blessings the Lord pours out upon His faithful senior couples for their willingness to sacrifice in moving forward the great cause of Zion. Why not put the Lord to the test?

Chapter 5

DO WE HAVE TO PROSELYTE?

One of the questions asked most often by those considering a mission is, do we have to proselyte, knock doors, and otherwise try to keep up with the younger missionaries? The answer has been clearly spelled out by our leaders. Elder David B. Haight said: "It is not necessary for you to proselyte in the same way as our young elders and sisters. Couples are often among the most fruitful missionaries because of their maturity, seasoned experience, insight, and compassion that open many doors in an unusual way. . . . Sister Shawcroft recommends that every couple take on their mission a good chocolate chip cookie recipe, lots of love, a good recipe for cinnamon rolls, a strong testimony of the gospel, the scriptures, and then more love!"[1]

One of your talents that most young missionaries have not yet developed is the talent to slow down and appreciate the journey, still anticipating the destination. Senior sisters thrilled new members and investigators by demonstrating what is second nature to them but was totally foreign to their students. Even baking cookies, which everyone except the grandchildren often take for granted, was a total amazement to new members. Many senior elders took time to teach investigators how to tie ties, play the harmonica, or play checkers. Although there is much to do and so precious little time to do it, many young missionaries fail to appreciate the value of engaging in activities that will strengthen their investigators when the missionaries can no longer spend time with them daily.

There are multitudes of other assignments that are not generally filled by younger missionaries, for which couples are well suited. Elder Jacob de Jager said: "However, there is still the mistaken idea among many couples that their missionary work would be proselyting only. I hope by what I have just said that they now have a better insight and will reconsider the possibility of service, especially when they hear that, contrary to the established policy for other callings in the kingdom, they can come forward and express their desire to go on a six-, twelve-, or eighteen-month mission."[2]

Some of the other possibilities for service include being called as office missionaries. Without our office missionaries, we would not have survived. Often a senior sister served as the secretary to the president while her husband was the "car czar"—in charge of the car reports, servicing and maintaining the fleet, checking mileage, and so on. It was very comforting to me for a senior couple to serve as the financial secretaries and referral secretaries. Their thoroughness and attention to detail often kept us out of hot water with Salt Lake. Their conscientiousness far exceeded the limited attention span of the vast majority of younger missionaries.

In many missions there is a crying need for health and welfare missionaries who can teach what we consider to be second nature skills but are not evident to the local people. Some senior elders who have engaged all of their lives in farming are answers to prayers for the local people who desperately need their farming skills and know-how just to survive physically.

The Church posts on seniormissionary.churchofjesuschrist.org requests for education missionaries who can assist in setting up seminaries and institutes in the expanding areas of the Church where professional Church Education System personnel cannot be assigned. You may feel woefully lacking because you have never been a professional teacher—that is, until you arrive and see that the limited talents you have so far exceed anything that is available locally that you are viewed as an angel from heaven. Just your experience in attending Sunday School and priesthood or Relief Society over the years has equipped you for your assignment far beyond what you may now understand. You may be asked to participate in the worldwide Pathway program to supervise and monitor students preparing to begin their college career. The teaching is done online, but the "cheerleading" is done by senior missionaries—where available. I am just completing a course on Foundations of the Restoration taught from home to students in Australia on Zoom.

Both elders and sisters (of the senior variety) are in high demand to teach leadership skills to the newly converted Saints. Again, you may think that if you haven't been a bishop or Relief Society president that you are not qualified. There isn't a person reading this book who couldn't organize a sacrament meeting properly based on the number of meetings they have attended over the years. The basics of giving assignments and following up to see that everything is done is a skill you could teach without having to have an advanced degree in organizational behavior from a university.

Teaching children and adults to read and write is also an assignment you may enjoy. Materials will be provided for you to help you approach your assignment in an organized, systematic manner. The joy you see in the eyes of elderly men and women when you hand them a Book of Mormon and they realize they can actually read it is beyond our ability to describe. The letters you will receive in their childlike pen hand when you return home will fill your hearts with love and appreciation for years to come. Your family may be a little baffled with your tears when they read the letters and fail to see what is so touching about those elementary words. But you will know how far your friends have come and how much joy you have helped bring into their lives. In many missions you may be asked by the mission president to teach non-English speaking missionaries how to speak, read, and write English. It will change their lives forever.

If you haven't experienced it yourself, it is difficult to fully comprehend what we are saying. Having been there and experienced the joy, it is difficult to put into words the thrill you will receive as you tackle the monsters of ignorance and illiteracy.

You may be asked to help the people with genealogy and family history matters. The new converts are so excited about the entire gospel program that you will likely sense a feeling of shame that we, in the central stakes, are so complacent about the blessings we enjoy. Watching their eyes light up as you help them complete their family group sheets, or prepare names for temple work, or find a lost ancestor will thrill you much more than watching yet another athletic competition, play, or musical production. Until you have been embraced by a three-hundred-pound convert and danced around the family history center in childlike joy because you helped him find the missing link in his family tree, it is difficult to imagine how the feelings you are experiencing supersede the feelings you get at a family dinner with the grandchildren. All you have to do is talk to someone who has experienced the heavenly joy of Christ-like service and, even though you may not still fully comprehend what they are saying, you will be assured that what we are writing is fact.

You may be called as a "shadow leader" to the branch president who has been a member of the Church less than a year. Enthusiasm they have. Experience they have not. That is where you come in. Something as simple as conducting a meeting scares the new convert. As you stand by his or her side and tell them what to say, as you help them prepare and follow a simple agenda, as you move away unnoticed as they continue to conduct the meeting, there is a sense of heavenly joy that just plain defies description. Perhaps watching your children or grandchildren take their first unaided steps comes closest to the feelings you will have.

Teaching Primary with a dozen little faces glowing at you as you struggle to make the gospel simple enough for them to understand leaves one with an appreciation difficult to describe. Teaching teenagers who are actually eager to listen, learn, and participate may restore your confidence in the youth of today. Teaching new converts to lead the singing, say a public prayer, or bless a child seems so elementary to us but so revelatory to them.

Elder Hugh W. Pinnock continues the spirit of this chapter by saying:

> There is so much for you to do in the mission field, either as a couple or, if you do not have a mate, as an elder or sister missionary. It is true, you will not be tracting quite like the younger missionaries, or at least

> not as long, but you will be influencing the inactive, providing welfare service instruction, serving in our visitors centers, meeting the town fathers, and helping those that need your leadership example, your judgment, and your ability to teach. Investigators in Stuttgart, West Germany; Hermosillo, Mexico; Williamsport, Pennsylvania; and Rocky Ford, Colorado, will listen and, yes, be baptized because of you.[3]

It almost seems impossible that everything we have talked about in this chapter could actually happen to you. This is only the tip of the iceberg. In a million different ways, the things we take for granted will become so real in the lives of these wonderful, humble converts. Once you have seen for yourself the power of senior couples, you will appreciate the enthusiasm the mission presidents have when they get the news that another couple is coming to serve with them.

There is one aspect of service that will be similar to that experienced with the younger missionaries. You will not escape the notice of the adversary and his demonic followers. The amount of good you will do is so great that he cannot afford to ignore it. Therefore, there will be challenges and trials in the mission field. It's nothing that you cannot overcome with the help of the Lord, but it would be unrealistic to expect that a mission will be easy or a bed of roses. As you discover the magnitude of the task ahead of you, it is normal to face feelings of discouragement and inadequacy. However, the needs were there before you arrived, and they will be there long after you have gone. Just do the best you can do and leave the rest in the hands of the Lord.

A word of caution. After you have arrived, settled into your assignment, and seen how much work there is to do, don't become angry with your friends back home who haven't yet responded to the call of the prophet. It is good to write them encouraging letters and invite them to join you, but be cautious about harshly condemning them for not serving. We marvel at how patient the Lord is with us when we fail to have the same vision He has about the true meaning of life and what is of most importance. Perhaps we should exercise the same patience toward our friends and loved ones who haven't yet (but hopefully, will!) catch the same contagious vision you now have.

The Lord established the criteria for service in His kingdom: "Therefore, O ye that embark in the service of God, see that ye serve him with all your heart, might, mind and strength, that ye may stand blameless before God at the last day. Therefore, if ye have desires to serve God ye are called to the work" (D&C 4:2–3).

The Lord wants sons and daughters who are willing to serve with all their heart. That doesn't require a college degree. He wants all of our might, doing as much as we can with as much vigor and determination as we can muster. Still no college degree required. Next He wants our minds. Even with this prerequisite the Lord does not specify a certain IQ. He just wants us to use what He has blessed us with and has promised to make up whatever deficit there is. He wants us to give what strength we have. Some are in good health and can do more. Some are required by diminishing strength and health to take a more conservative approach to the work. The Lord does not specify the level of physical output He requires, only that we serve with all of our strength.

Further in that great missionary section, the Lord specifies in list form the qualifications for His workers and then broadens the list to those who really want to excel. He said: "And faith, hope, charity and love, with an eye single to the glory of God, qualify him for the work. Remember faith, virtue, knowledge, temperance, patience, brotherly kindness, godliness, charity, humility, diligence" (D&C 4:5–6).

What does it mean to serve with "an eye single to the glory of God?" You will recall when the Lord revealed to Moses the grand design in creating and peopling this earth he said: "For behold, this is my work and my glory—to bring to pass the immortality and eternal life of man" (Moses 1:39). So, whenever we labor with our objective to help improve and exalt our brothers and sisters, we are serving with an eye single to His glory.

As you review those traits listed in verses 5 and 6 above, you may notice that a similar list is found in 2 Peter 1:5–10 as that ancient apostle urged the Saints to "make their calling and election sure." By doing the works of the Father in the manner prescribed in Doctrine and Covenants 4:5–6, we are step-by-step making our calling and election sure. Then we will never fail. How gracious the Lord is to allow us all to serve in our own way, according to the talents He had blessed us with, and according to the speed we are physically capable of.

If there are other questions about what is required of senior couples, talk to someone who has been on a mission. Call the missionary committee at Church Headquarters and ask them directly the questions you may have that we haven't touched upon. For your convenience, here is the contact information: 1–800–453–3860, ext. 2–6741, or email seniormissionaryservices@churchofjesuschrist.org.

It is too easy to listen to those who have not gone on missions spread their gloom and doom logic as justification for not going. It is infinitely more productive to ask those who have or are now serving and see it from their perspective.

As we approach the final scenes before the Second Coming of the Savior, it is imperative that we all do everything within our power to prepare the earth for that blessed event. There will always be negative, dissenting voices pointing out the impossibility of the job or our own personal inadequacies. However, whom the Lord calls, He qualifies. Let's give Him a chance to make of us what He knows we are capable of becoming.

NOTES

1. David B. Haight, *Ensign*, May 1987, 60–61.
2. Jacob de Jager, *Ensign*, May 1981, 12.
3. Hugh W. Pinnock, *Ensign*, November 1979, 74–75.

Chapter 6
HEALTH CONCERNS

Incident to the aging process is the escalating of health concerns. The questions are endless, the answers are precious few. Because the future has not yet happened, there will always be a question mark about what our state of health will be in the future. One of the traps the adversary seems to successfully place in our way is the fear of the unknown. A person can waste an entire lifetime worrying about something that never materializes. I call it building bridges across chasms only to discover that there is no chasm when we arrive at our bridge. All of our efforts have been wasted in worrying about a possible condition over which we have no control.

Worrying about the "what ifs" of life is of limited value. You learned many years ago that in the divinely revealed decision-making process, a person was required to list the pros and cons of each proposal. Not as well understood is the procedure for choosing between two or more possible alternatives. It is wise to still make two columns of pros and cons on a single sheet of paper. Then compare lists. If the positive on one list is a negative on the other list, then that factor counts. If a negative on one list is also a negative on the other list, then that factor doesn't count. Perhaps an example would illustrate the point we are trying to make.

Suppose you have a bad case of asthma. The two columns you are trying to decide upon are (1) going on a mission or (2) staying home.

If you would have asthma whether you went on a mission or not (asthma is a negative on both lists), then you wouldn't count that as a weighty factor. If you lived in a cold climate and your body reacted adversely during times of winter, that would be a negative factor on the "stay home" list. If you were called to serve in a warm, temperate climate, that would be a plus factor on the "go on a mission" list. Can you see how that works?

If you are spending $1,000 a month on fixed expenses and the mission costs $1,000 a month, then whether you stay or go really doesn't make that much difference. If you are conscientious in making your lists and honestly evaluating the pros and cons, it will become evident that going on a mission is about as safe as staying home.

If you have known medical challenges, make sure you list them on the missionary recommendation form. The Brethren who make the assignments are very sensitive to the health needs of the senior couples. Before submitting your papers, you both are required to have a thorough physical examination. The form is included in the packet of papers you receive from the bishop at the time you indicate your desire to serve. If you are savvy enough, all of the forms are online (your grandchildren can help you call them up). If there are health concerns, the doctor will note them on the medical form along with his recommendations indicating any limitations he would impose on your service.

As you make your appointment with the doctor, make sure to schedule enough time to ask whatever questions or concerns you may have. It would be to your advantage to keep a note pad with you for a week or two before the physical so you can jot down your questions. Too many couples reported that they had a whole shopping list of questions for the doctor until he asked: "Do either of you have any questions?" Then their minds went blank. A poor note pad is better than a good memory.

Depending on which country you are assigned to, there will be a number of preventative inoculations. If you are diligent in getting them, the chance of you contracting some strange and unknown disease is slim. If you have a question, for example, when the last tetanus booster you had, better be safe than sorry—get another one. The

Church is very concerned that they protect and preserve the health of the missionaries.

Depending on what you report on the medical form, you may be limited to where you can serve. If at all possible, leave the assignment up to the Lord and His servants. Too many couples set limits on where they will serve. Some dear friends of ours decided that they absolutely did not want to serve in Africa. They so noted on the recommendation form. They were both physically fit with no limitations. Perhaps the Lord was trying to teach them that His will was to be done rather than their own. They opened the call and read South Africa Johannesburg Mission and nearly passed away.

Because of their faithfulness, they went on their mission in spite of their misgivings. When they returned home they admitted that the Lord knew best. To this day they speak in very glowing terms about their wonderful mission to South Africa. Neither of them had any health problems, they were completely safe, and they made some of the dearest friends of their entire lives. When asked if they regretted going, their answer is always a resounding "no."

If you do have limitations imposed by your health, do not despair. There is a need wherever you are called to serve. We served as mission president in California. The couples who served with us were from all over the United States and Canada. None of them looked at their assignment with anything other than total excitement. Even those couples who had served in foreign missions said that California compared favorably with their foreign missions. It truly is not where you serve that makes the difference.

The better physical shape you can both be in when you enter the MTC (Missionary Training Center), the better off you will be. As soon as the decision to serve has been made, start a regular, sensible exercise program if you don't have one already. Going on a mission is a wonderful excuse for taking off the ten or twenty pounds you have been promising to lose for the past several years. If you are terribly overweight, your opportunity to serve may have to be postponed until corrective measures are taken. At the very least, a three-to-five-mile walk a day would do wonders for your cardiovascular well-being. Start slowly and work up. If you start too quickly into hard physical exercise, your muscles will become stiff and sore, and you are not too likely to continue your "getting in shape" program.

Some couples participate in water aerobics because it is not as hard on aging joints yet offers more resistance than just walking. Other couples decide to swim a few laps at the local pool. If you are sent to a mission where the altitude differs greatly from your home altitude, you will find yourself sleepy most of the time for the first few weeks until your body adjusts to the different elevation. The better shape you are in, the easier the transition into missionary life.

If there are elective surgeries you should take care of before your mission, get them done now. Taking time out in the mission field to recover from minor surgery is a terrible waste of the Lord's time. It's better to take care of those issues at home where children and grandchildren can nurse you back to full health. Having taken care of those items, you will be less likely to stress out as you get serious about sending in your papers.

If you have chronic problems that have plagued you for many years, consider consulting a doctor. Such great strides have been made during the past decade that procedures which were impossible a few years ago are standard procedures today. Perhaps you will be pleasantly surprised that some minor surgery will completely restore your health even before the Resurrection.

Many seniors have a shopping list of medications they are taking. Before submitting your papers, consult your doctor and determine if all of the medications are absolutely necessary. If they are, see how many can be purchased in bulk sufficient to last you for the year or eighteen months you are gone. For those prescriptions that cannot be given for that long a period, have the doctor write a prescription that your children or a trusted neighbor can have filled and sent to you before you run out of the medication you took with you. Many pharmacies will send the medication directly to you at your request. Check around and get your procedures lined up before you leave. The more "little details" you can address before you leave, the less likely that neighbors, friends, or family will have to make a crisis move to avert a calamity in the mission field. Many places where senior missionaries are assigned have modern pharmacies that can fill your prescriptions.

Many doctors are familiar with missionaries going into the field. Many have a generous reduction in their fees (some even donate their services free!) for those who are called to serve. You might want to check around and see if there is a doctor who is so inclined. The same is true of dentists. Many doctors and dentists provided free services to our missionaries while they were serving. We didn't expect it of them, they just volunteered. The irony was that many of the doctors who donated free services were not members of the Church.

If the combination of your health record and your doctor's recommendation eliminates a certain part of the world, take it like a mature adult. It would not be a sign of maturity to call up the missionary committee of the Church and argue either for or against an assignment to a certain place. You will discover within the first few months in the field why you were sent to the mission you were assigned to. Almost without exception, the couples would meet someone or baptize someone who seems so familiar there must have been a bond established before coming to earth. With each couple who valiantly served, it was evident why they had been assigned to our mission. The reasons were varied, but there was always a reason. That shouldn't surprise us since the Lord never does anything by chance.

If the doctor concludes that it is not advisable for you to serve, don't despair. There is always work to be done at home in the temples, in the family history centers, and so on. Judging from some of the physical wrecks (but spiritual masterpieces!) we had sent to us, almost anyone who really wants to serve can be called. There are even full-time missions where you can stay at home and serve in your local area.

One word of caution. Because it is a proven fact that health diminishes with age, the longer you wait to serve, the more likely you'll experience some health problems. With the passage of time, the reasons for you to vacillate increase. If you wait too long, you will talk yourself out of serving even if your health doesn't preclude you from going. What a tragedy if you postpone making the decision until it is too late. What compensatory event would have to take place to replace the experiences you missed in the mission field? No one can tell. If you hurry and fill out your papers now, you will never have to find out the disappointment of the dilatory.

So many of our couples said their health actually improved in the mission field. With one of our particularly loved couples, the wife had a brain tumor. Her husband had jokingly told me he wouldn't go across the street to a dog fight with her in that bad of condition. They served faithfully among the Hmong people and extended from a year to a year and a half. During the entire time in California, she never suffered from ill health. Almost from the day they went home, her health returned to its former compromised state. They have often said the worst thing they did was leave the mission field.

You will never know how the Lord can bless you health-wise unless you exercise enough faith to put Him to the test. You have so much to give. Don't let a few aches and pains keep you from having the greatest experience of your entire lives. The Lord promises that He will sanctify you by the Spirit unto the renewing of your bodies (see D&C 84:33). He also said: "And any man [or woman] that shall go and preach this gospel of the kingdom, and fail not to continue faithful in all things, shall not be weary in mind, neither darkened, neither in body, limb, nor joint; and a hair of his head shall not fall to the ground unnoticed. And they shall not go hungry, neither athirst" (D&C 84:80).

We would not be so bold in making the promise if we had not seen it work time and time again. The Lord is waiting to bless you. Don't keep Him waiting.

Chapter 7

LEARNING A NEW LANGUAGE

Is it veritably true that an old dog can't learn new tricks? If it is, someone forgot to tell the senior couples that. Every day couples are teaching the gospel in foreign languages that they did not know until they entered the MTC.

Many couples, however, even when they are sent to foreign speaking missions, do not learn the language. President Spencer W. Kimball told how it is being done: "The young missionaries are learning the difficult Navajo language, and the older couples are using largely the language of love."[1] That is not to say that there will not be some frustrations. Every one of our couples (most of whom labored among the Southeast Asians) learned to effectively communicate with their beloved people, but none of them mastered the language.

Elder Robert L. Backman, long associated with the missionary program as a member of the Seventy, said:

> Some have an idea that as we get older we can't learn languages. That is not true. Again and again, we see couples come to the Missionary Training Center without prior knowledge of a language and leave two months later able to communicate. Of course their skills increase as they love and serve in the mission field. Even when a new language is difficult, older couples perform a unique service in the missions simply by being there. Their experience, example, and faith serve as tremendous resources in building inexperienced members of the Church. They are

> absolutely indispensable to the growth of the kingdom across the world. I remember meeting a wonderful couple who were missionaries among the Southeast Asians of the California Oakland Mission. As I saw the bonding between the missionaries and these delightful new Latter-day Saints, I asked the sister missionary whether she could speak their language. She responded that she could not. I then asked her how they communicated with the members. With tears in her eyes, she replied, "We just love them."[2]

Every one of our couples learned at least the common greetings in the language they were assigned to work in. Others exerted more effort and learned to pray or bless the food in that language. Some senior couples devoted sufficient time to become fairly proficient in the language. They always had the young elders and sisters to help them out if they encountered a person who didn't speak or understand any English. We watched them teach occasionally. By the use of pictures, elementary language, and a lot of the Spirit and love, they were able to communicate on a level that needed no apology. Since our mission was a state-side mission, it was expected that the Southeast Asians would learn to speak English. Some couples spent a certain amount of time each week teaching them to speak English.

Very often our senior couples would identify a young person who was bilingual. They would solicit their help wherever the teaching required. This had a doubly positive effect. First, the family with limited English skills were taught in their native tongue; and second, the interpreter learned the gospel better and better as they were required to translate from English to their native tongue, as well as answer questions from the investigators. Many times these interpreters were not members of the Church to begin with. With the passage of time, almost all of them were eventually baptized. The Lord really does work in mysterious ways, His wonders to perform. Before we watched the interpreters at work, we did not understand how the Lord would allow everyone to hear the gospel in their own tongue. The Lord has promised, however: "For it shall come to pass in that day, that every man shall hear the fulness of the gospel in his own tongue, and in his own language, through those who are ordained unto this power, by the administration of the Comforter, shed forth upon them for the revelation of Jesus Christ" (D&C 90:11).

What if you are called to teach in a foreign language? Will you be able to learn to speak well enough so the people can understand? The answer to both questions is yes. Yes, you very well may be called to teach in a foreign language. And yes, the Lord will loosen your tongues and will quicken the ears of those you teach until you enjoy a high level of communication.

How does one go about learning a language? The MTC is wonderful at giving you a head start. There are just a few other tricks that may be helpful. Start as soon as you know which language you are going to speak and how to sound out the letters, reading from the Book of Mormon. We have never seen anything as effective at teaching language as well as converting as the Book of Mormon. Next, get some three-by-five cards. Write down key words and study them until they become part of your usable vocabulary. As you become more proficient, write the phrases in English you want to be able to say in your new language. Have a seasoned speaker translate it for you. Even better, have a local native speaker help you with the phrases. I discovered during my first mission to Samoa that the natives could understand me better when one of their own had taught me how to enunciate the words and construct the phrases. The American elders understood more of the grammar and word structure, but the natives spoke more fluently. In other words, the American missionaries can tell you "what," but the Native people can tell you "how".

If you will learn a new phrase every day for two months, you will be almost conversant in the language. If you can memorize ten new words a day, within that same two-month period, you will have a workable vocabulary. I took a leaf from Le Grand Richards' practice. He had been assigned to the Netherlands to speak Dutch. However, because of his clerical abilities, he had been assigned to the mission office where only English was spoken. Because of his intense desire to learn the language, he said he talked to every child, every dog, and every tree he saw until his ears became proficient at hearing his own voice say the words.

For anyone who has attempted to learn a new language, you will know that it is a lot easier to silently read the words to yourself in your own mind than it is to say them out loud. It seems like your tongue just keeps tripping over your teeth during those early days. In learning a language one of the most critical factors is learning how to laugh at yourself. It doesn't do any good to get mad at yourself or frustrated because you can't remember a word or phrase. When the native people laugh *at* you, they are really laughing *with* you. They are pleased and honored that you will attempt to learn their language.

Consistently using small islands of time is better than cramming using large blocks of time. Set up a reasonable schedule and practice daily. At first you will be sure you can never learn the language. Don't fall into the satanic trap of engaging in negative self-talk. If you tell yourself you will never learn the language, you will likely become a self-fulfilling prophecy. Whether you think you can or you can't, you are right.

After a couple of months of serious trying to learn the Samoan language, I discovered a very alarming phenomenon. In Samoan they call it "gu gu," which means "incapable of intelligent conversation." I had almost lost my ability to speak and think in English. I couldn't yet speak fluently in Samoan. I was "gu gu!" Thankfully, that stage passed and before the end of my mission I was fairly fluent in both Samoan and English. Others have reported similar experiences in other languages. If you know it is likely to happen, don't panic. Just laugh and keep trying. Eventually you will amaze even yourselves as you rattle off some phrase that just comes out naturally even though you really hadn't stop to think about it. It is called the gift of tongues and is given by the Lord frequently to His missionaries. Since the gift of tongues is one of the gifts of the Spirit mentioned in Doctrine and Covenants 46, you may expect to receive it to one degree or another as long as you live well enough to qualify for the Spirit.

When our oldest daughter was serving in the France Paris Mission, she was struggling with the French language. She persistently tried but sometimes just couldn't find the right word. As she tried to hunt for the word, her investigators would often supply the correct word. She then discovered that the people were actually bearing their testimony to her as they filled in the words. As they filled in the correct French words, the Spirit bore witness to them that what they were saying was true. Even after she became more proficient in the language, she would often have the investigators fill in the right words for her.

Could the same thing happen for your investigators? Another way of saying it might be, "Is anything too hard for the Lord?" (See Genesis 18:14; Jeremiah 32:27.) Don't wait until you are fluent in the language to speak it—if you do, you will never speak it. Part of the humbling process seems to be learning to take the ribbing that the other missionaries, members, and investigators give you as you struggle with the language.

There is another powerful manifestation of the Spirit that you might expect. It is called the interpretation of tongues. You may be teaching and speaking in English to an audience who does not speak English. Even though you may be working through an interpreter, you may discover that the people are correcting the interpreter when he doesn't do an adequate job of translating. Such was the case in a stake conference where Elder Hugh B. Brown was visiting many years ago in Samoa. I was familiar with both English and Samoan at the time he visited. It was a hot, muggy afternoon, and this was long before air conditioning was installed in any of our chapels. President Brown started to speak and became a little frustrated with the cumbersomeness of the translation process. He asked the translator if he would just take some notes and then summarize at the end of the meeting.

I got so caught up in his address that I didn't realize that no one was interpreting. At the conclusion of President Brown's talk, the interpreter stood to summarize. As I listened to him, I noticed he made several errors. I was about to raise my hand when other people started correcting him. I knew these people and knew that they did not speak English, so there wasn't a way they could have understood President Brown's message to the point they could correct the interpreter. After several attempts by the translator, and several corrections by the audience, he turned to President Brown and explained what was happening. He said, "I don't think these people need me to interpret. They seem to understand perfectly well your message."

President Brown responded, "You are correct. You needn't translate any further." I had just witnessed a true miracle.

Since that time, we have seen several instances when in interviews the people understood the questions without the help of an interpreter. If it could happen with President Brown, and it could happen to us, why not to you? It can and it will! Although you may have some serious questions about your ability to learn a foreign language, this should not deter you from filling out your papers and sending them in. Remember 2 Timothy 1:7: "For God has not given us the spirit of fear, but of power and of love and of a sound mind." Surely the Lord who called you on this mission and understands how to speak all languages will not leave you in a helpless situation. He will stand by you and help you develop every talent—including a new language, if necessary—you need to succeed.

NOTES

1. Spencer W. Kimball, *Improvement Era*, December 1960, 923.
2. Robert L. Backman, *Ensign*, November 1992, 14.

Chapter 8

CUSTOMS, CULTURES, AND OUR AGING SYSTEMS

If you have traveled very much, you are aware that there is a wide variety of customs from land to land. I had my first real awakening as a young missionary in Samoa. I had been sitting cross-legged on mats covering crushed corral floors. Not being accustomed to that cramped condition, my legs started to rebel after a couple of hours. Innocently I straightened my legs out to restart the circulation of blood. Immediately my senior companion poked me and told me never to point the bottoms of my feet toward anybody. I asked why and he explained that in their custom it was very offensive because it sent the message that the people I had extended my feet toward were considered less than the dust beneath my feet. I certainly didn't intend that message to be sent; I was just trying to ease the pain in my legs. I asked him how I was to accomplish my objective without offending them. He explained that I could either tuck my feet toward the rear of the fale (home), or I could cover my feet with a mat. The problem was not unsolvable, but I needed to learn that certain gestures that mean little or nothing in the United States can have very serious repercussions in other lands.

The whole Church was sensitized to the cultural differences a number of years ago when two missionaries, in a thoughtless, teenage gesture, climbed on top of a statue of Buddha in Thailand to have their pictures taken. Not realizing (or not respecting) the sacredness of that statue cost them some time in jail and set back the missionary work by many years. Had they been aware or serious about the local customs, they would have taken whatever steps were necessary to avoid offending the very people they had been sent there to teach.

Seldom do local customs go against Church standards. The offense usually occurs when missionaries have not traveled extensively enough or are not sensitive enough to be aware of the implications of their actions. So, as quickly as you learn of your assignment, contact someone who has served in that country or a native of the country who is living near you. Ask them pointed questions about their customs. Your mission president may send you information that will help you get a feel for different customs. At most universities, there is a department or a part of the library that deals with international affairs. They have two- or three-page handouts that summarize the size, population, geography, and some customs of each country. We found them very helpful to understand the Southeast Asian people even though they were living in California.

If you are unable to obtain help before your mission, at least you will be sensitized to the need to learn about their customs when you arrive. If you haven't discovered it already, you will soon learn that many customs, if adopted in America, would make us a much more polite, easy-to-live-with people. Unfortunately, in many places in the world, people's impression of America has been molded by thoughtless travelers who seem to have little or no regard for anyone other than themselves. When you watch how many American visitors act, you may feel anger welling up inside of you at their total lack of courtesy. I was so embarrassed with one group of American tourists who visited Samoa during my first mission that I actually spoke with an Australian brogue so they wouldn't associate me with the American tourists.

Learning new customs and cultures is one of the truly pleasant parts of missionary work. You will discover some differences that make you uncomfortable until you understand them. For example, in the United States our conversational distance is about two feet. If people stand much farther away, we want to move forward because we feel like we're having to yell to make them hear. In many parts of the world, the conversational distance is much closer. For the first month in Samoa, I found myself unconsciously backing away from the people. They kept advancing closer to me. An astute missionary pointed out my behavior and explained that their conversational distance is anywhere from six inches to a foot closer than ours. I felt like they were trying to kiss me; they felt like I was too distant to speak to. I held my ground, and to my surprise, they didn't kiss me. They stopped between eighteen inches and a foot from my face.

Once I became accustomed to it, I was perfectly comfortable. The problem came when I returned home. I had become "Samoanized" and kept advancing closer to the people I was talking to because I felt they were too far away. We had a lot of good laughs before I was able to return to the American way.

After being home for more than fifty years from my Samoan mission, I still find it difficult to talk to a person when they are sitting down without crouching down myself. That is the Samoan way, and I like it. In Samoa, if a person agrees with you, they don't say anything. It has taken me many years to remember to respond if I agree. It isn't easy to switch back and forth from one culture to another without making some mistakes.

In some countries the people hold on to a handshake while they talk with you. It was very uncomfortable for me at first. They really aren't trying to make a pass at you or do anything inappropriate. That is just the way their culture does things. The list can go on endlessly. You can learn most quickly by being aware and keeping your eyes open. Watch how others interact. Most people are very understanding when you make social mistakes based on differences in customs. However, it does not speak well for us if we never try to learn not to offend because of ignorance or disrespect for their local customs. Don't let the fear of learning something new dissuade you from going on a mission. You will love what you learn from the local people.

Perhaps more challenging than the customs and cultural differences you will face will be the foods that are so foreign to your palate. If you are confined to a rather strict diet by your doctor, then there isn't much question what you should do. However, if it is just a matter of taste or personal preference, you may want to reconsider your choice. In many parts of the world, the local people will give you the very best that they have even though they cannot afford it or even if their own children must go without. It would be an offense of the first order for you to refuse something that they have sacrificed a month's food budget to purchase.

As you become familiar with the local people, you can let them know before the situation arises that you are on a restricted diet and, therefore, there are many things you cannot eat. They will generally respect that and will not be offended when you must decline their generous offer.

In Samoa they practice the kava ceremony. The kava is made from the roots of a native plant. If not strictly forbidden by the Word of Wisdom, it probably should be. It tasted very much like spiked, dirty dish water—to me. The drink was prepared in the presence of all of the invited guests. Then it was ladled from a bowl in a coconut shell cup and passed to each person. Everyone took a sip and passed it on. If you happened to be sitting near the end of the line, most of what you got was back wash! Not a very appetizing thought! To refuse the kava would have been very offensive. Therefore, we would put the cup to our lips, tilt it up as though we were drinking, and pass the cup on. No one ever said anything about being offended.

In discussing with our senior couples how they got around some of the Southeast Asian food they were served in California, many said they would take just a bite or two and leave the rest. Wouldn't that be offensive? Usually not because the children eat whatever is remaining on your plate. Therefore, the more you eat the less they get to eat. A token sampling of their food is generally sufficient to satisfy their customs.

A note of caution: if you see little children sitting in the shadows watching you eat, it generally means that they only get the remains. Even if the food is delicious and there seems to be plenty of it, be conservative in how much you eat. I learned this the hard way in Samoa. We were in the middle of a famine season because our food supply had been destroyed by a hurricane. A family invited us over for supper. They laid out a spread that resembled a feast for a king. I thought I was starving, so immediately after the blessing on the food, I dove into my plate. I had only taken a few bites when my companion nudged me and told me I was full. I protested that I had only begun the meal. He gestured toward the children. It didn't long before it dawned on me what he was saying. I pushed the plate away. They urged me to eat more. I told them I'd had enough. The kids came out and retrieved the plate and devoured it in a minute. I really wasn't as hungry as I thought I had been.

Some drinks are obviously against the Word of Wisdom. You may politely decline and then when questioned, you can teach them about the Word of Wisdom. Even if they don't agree with you, they will respect your refusal based on religious beliefs. The more difficult situations come when something is against your personal word of wisdom but not specifically forbidden by the Lord. You may have strong feelings about cola drinks. In many places, the only drinks they serve are caffeinated drinks. You must deal with this problem on a personal basis. It would be well to determine what you will do before the situation arises.

When you were younger your constitution may have been like steel. Nothing phased it. As we get older, it often becomes a fact that our systems can't tolerate everything we used to eat. Unfortunately, you will generally discover by sad experience what foods your system can and cannot tolerate. Be very cautious about eating pork. In many countries if the pork is cooked at all it is merely passed over the flames. There is no need to sacrifice your health by eating something that would make you ill under the best of circumstances.

It is true that the Lord will protect you even from poisonous food if you ingest it innocently. However, to tempt Him by eating something we know is bad may result in some rather serious physical repercussions. It isn't any fun to be tethered to the bathroom for a couple of days while the offending food works through the system. Often the newness of the food causes gastrointestinal problems while our systems adjust.

Generally, after a few weeks to a couple of months, our systems settle down and we don't experience the same problems we may have experienced when we first arrived. Take along a supply of antacids, diarrhea medicine, and laxatives. Even if you are fortunate enough not to need them, there may be other senior couples or even young missionaries who will be forever grateful for your having a supply.

In the remote event that your system will not adjust to the food, give the mission president a call. He will contact a team of medical doctors in Salt Lake City and they will prescribe whatever medicine is necessary to help you through the rough times. If that doesn't work, you will likely be transferred to another mission where the food resembles more what you are accustomed to. Be assured that neither the Lord nor the mission president wants to see you suffer because of food problems.

Generally, the mission president will warn you before giving you an assignment whether you need to peel all fruits and vegetables. Other senior couples may even be more helpful than the mission president in warning you about local foods. It is not generally necessary to take a supply of food with you on your mission. However, if there is something you really like and wonder whether it is available in your mission, give the mission office a call and they will tell you.

Thankfully, you will discover that the kingdom of God is more than meat and drink. Although the items mentioned in this chapter are helpful and should be considered, you will find that food concerns are far from the top of your list of things to be concerned about.

Chapter 9

THE MTC EXPERIENCE

There have been so many stories circulated about the Mission Training Center that we thought rather than give you our own impressions, we would ask people who were currently going through it. Before doing that, however, we will say that the reactions vary from thinking they have died and gone to heaven to thinking they have died and gone to the other place. You will find the same varied responses to the MTC as you will find in work, in Church, or in life in general. Why would we expect it to be any different?

Many couples report that they have never experienced such a continuous string of "spiritual highs" in their lives. From the moment you arrive, you talk, study, learn, listen, eat, drink, and sleep gospel. Although the hours spent in classroom learning activities are difficult, they are not impossible. Don't be afraid to make your instructor aware of any personal needs, such as a rest break. Remember, the mind can only absorb as much as the seat can endure. Take some stand-up breaks often enough to ensure good circulation of blood. For those of you who are not accustomed to long sessions of study, you may find staying awake during the classes challenging. Do not despair. That does not mean you are not interested or spiritually insensitive. It takes a while to get into studying shape. It will come with time.

There will be times of discouragement. Especially is this true if you are learning a language. Your tongue will get tangled up on your teeth and you'll think you sound like a little child first learning to talk. Don't worry about it. If the Lord wanted you to speak fluently from the day you arrived, He would have given you the unrestrained gift of tongues. Some miracles take a little longer than others. You may as well enjoy learning to hear your own voice speak a strange and foreign language. In time you will start to recognize words and phrases. Push yourselves. Learn as many new words each day as possible. Remember, everyone in your MTC district is in the same boat. You are not competing with each other. You are all trying to help each other succeed.

One of the problems noted by the couples was the food. They didn't complain that it was bad—there was just too much of it. Fighting the constant battle for weight gain was a problem for many couples. There were always the enviable exceptions. Some elder or sister who could eat as much as he or she wanted without gaining a pound. Most of the couples, however, did not fall into this favored category. We noticed couples walking every day we passed the Missionary Training Center. A good plan of exercise will help your circulation and will also help burn off the extra pounds you otherwise would pack away and carry to the mission field.

Many couples worried about being able to memorize. Unless you have been rather diligent throughout your lives in reading and studying scriptures, it is rather challenging to memorize scripture. You may find it more productive to try to remember the references to certain passages. Before too long, as you review them daily, you will discover that you not only remember where they are located by reference, but also where they are located on the page in your scriptures. Unfortunately, this is not an advantage enjoyed by those using electronic scriptures. After teaching scriptures for more than forty years, I still prefer to use my hard-copy scriptures. Yes, I do also have a smart phone that has my scriptures on it just in case I don't have my regular scriptures.

I taught scripture professionally for many years. It was always amazing to the students when I would say, "You'll find that passage in Alma chapter 5 on the left-hand page, right hand column half way down the page." They would all marvel as if I had a photographic memory. If I could remember, I would have told them the exact verse number. Location is a good secondary method.

We discovered a method years ago that really seemed to help remember passages. After reading a passage, ask yourself, "What question would someone have to ask so this passage of scripture would be the answer?" Perhaps a quick example will demonstrate the principles. In the early days of my first mission, I read the entire standard works from cover to cover (to compensate for my failure to diligently study during my growing up years). One particular day I read Doctrine and Covenants 6:16, which reads: "Yea, I tell thee, that thou mayest know that there is none else save God that knowest thy thoughts and the intents of thy heart." I determined that someone would have to ask if Satan could read our thoughts, to which, if they did ask, this verse would be the appropriate answer.

The very next day in proselyting, an investigator asked my companion that exact question. Since it was asked in Samoan (and I hadn't yet mastered the language), my companion had to translate. He didn't know the answer. The investigator seemed sincere in asking. I told him that I knew the answer. He sort of laughed at me and asked me what the answer was. Rather than give my own opinion (which meant absolutely nothing), I cited the scriptural reference. To their total amazement, the answer was there. From that day until now, I have never forgotten that verse. Once you use a scripture in a gospel discussion, it will be yours.

It is my goal never to use personal opinion to answer a difficult gospel question. Let the Lord give the answer. Amazingly, to almost every question I was ever asked by bright BYU students, the Lord gave a direct answer. It just required time and energy to learn them.

One way we used to learn passages of scriptures was to write them out on three-by-five cards. We would write the reference on one side of the card and the text of the verse on the other. Then several times during the day we would quiz ourselves and each other on the content of the verses. It was amazing how quickly the references started to stick.

The key seems to be learning how to learn. You will remember that the Lord said: "Whatever principle of intelligence we attain unto in this life, it will rise with us in the resurrection" (D&C 130:18). It isn't the amount of knowledge that seems to be the differentiating factor but the principle of how to acquire knowledge that gives one the advantage in this world and in the world to come.

You will not be required to memorize the discussions. You will be able to take the concepts and teach them in your own words. Your wisdom and experience will help you know what teaching style suits you best. Play to your strengths. One of our senior couples had worked on a ranch all their lives. They taught best by drawing analogies between principles of the gospel and working with livestock. The people they taught, although not ranchers, identified easily with the principles they were teaching.

Almost everyone at the MTC noted time and again the power of the Spirit they felt. You will be taught by General Authorities as well as young returned missionaries. The weekly devotionals were mentioned by all as being really memorable. Although you interface with the younger missionaries often, you are really being taught in groups of other senior couples. A second warning is in order: do not compete with each other. We are all on the Lord's team, and one is not better or worse than another. Feelings can get hurt if you constantly compare yourself with others. You may be particularly gifted in one area that is a real struggle for someone else. Conversely, you may really struggle with something that comes naturally to another missionary. Learn to glory in the success of each other, and we will be much closer to a Zion society. Remember the Lord's directive:

> Behold, here is wisdom also in me for your good. And you are to be equal, or in other words, you are to have equal claims on the properties, for the benefit of managing the concerns of your stewardships, every man according to his wants and his needs, inasmuch as his wants are just—And all this for the benefit of the church of the living God, that every man may improve upon his talent, that every man may gain other talents, yea, even an hundred fold, to be cast into the Lord's storehouse, to become the common property of the whole church—Every man seeking the interest of his neighbor, and doing all things with an eye single to the glory of God. (D&C 82:16–19)

Every talent we have is for the benefit of the Lord's Church. Therefore, when one excels we all profit thereby. Aren't we eternally grateful that the Prophet Joseph Smith was willing to use his talents to bless the entire world? What if the Savior had been selfish about using His limitless talents to bless all mankind? Do we all need to be saviors? Do we all need to be prophets of the Restoration? What progress we could make in the Church, and especially in missionary work, if we would just glory in each other's strengths and seek each other's interests.

You will make some of your dearest friends in the MTC. It is a tearful, but joyful, day when you leave the MTC and separate to your assigned fields of labor. Many couples carried on correspondence throughout their missions with friends they had made in the MTC. Reunions after the mission often were exchanging mission war stories.

Why do you become so attached in such a short period of time? Because these are people of like willingness to sacrifice their leisure to serve the Lord full-time. So why the attraction? Because in the gospel, likes attract. "For intelligence cleaveth unto intelligence; wisdom receiveth wisdom; truth embraceth truth; virtue loveth virtue; light cleaveth unto light; mercy hath compassion on mercy and claimeth her own; justice continueth its course and claimeth its own; judgment goeth before the face of him who sitteth upon the throne and governeth and executeth all things" (D&C 88:40).

Even your instructors in the MTC become like sons and daughters. They are selflessly sharing their talents to bless your lives, and an automatic bond is established. At times you may be frustrated at their apparent lack of understanding and compassion. Remember, they have been where you are going and have done what you will be doing and are doing everything in their power to prepare you for what is ahead. Don't be too harsh in criticizing them. When they are your age, they will see things differently. For now, they are doing the best they know how, given the maturity the Lord has blessed them with.

There are also temple excursions you will take while in the MTC. Weekly you will be allowed to take in a session at the Provo Temple, so be sure you take your current temple recommend. Many of the couples reported that the temple takes on a new and deeper meaning to them, even though many had been serving for years as temple officiators. You are entering a new experience, and so the temple takes on new meaning. That is just one of the many benefits of having everything in the temple presented symbolically. No one ever complained at having to go to the temple while in the MTC.

The excitement generated during those short weeks in the MTC will sustain you time and again in the early months in the mission field. The Lord sends you out with a full spiritual tank of gas into the field. It will be filled to overflowing many times in the mission field. However, there will be times you will need the reserve tank from the MTC to carry you through a particularly difficult time.

Some couples who are from areas not too distant from the MTC are permitted to return home to drop off surplus clothing, pick up items they have forgotten, and bid a final farewell to their families who want to see for themselves that Grandpa and Grandma are doing as well as their letters indicate. If you are going to a foreign mission, this may not be an option.

Chapter 10

FLYING OR DRIVING TO THE MISSION FIELD

This looks like a question that could be answered in a single statement. However, it is somewhat more complex than that. If you are assigned to a foreign mission, this may be a moot question. The Church does not expect you to ship your car across the ocean or have you purchase a car when you get there. In many remote missions, having a car is just not a consideration. Virtually all of your travel is made on foot or by public transportation.

For example, if you were assigned to London, England, you would not want to take a car. There are millions of people on the roadways, and they all seem to be going exactly where you are going. The "tube," or the intra-city subway system, is a wonderful thing. You can hop on the tube and be within easy walking distance of anywhere you need to go within a few minutes. The same is true with the Metro in Paris, France. In many of the major cities of the world, driving your car would not only be hazardous but so expensive it would be impractical. The mission president will provide you the direction on which way to go when you receive your call.

If your mission is in the United States or Canada, taking a car may be a matter of serious consideration. Let's review how missionaries move around, using our mission in Fresno, California, as an example. The Church gives each mission a "compliment" of cars. We had fifty-one cars assigned to our mission. That included a car for the president, a mission van, a mission truck, and forty-eight mission cars. With two hundred missionaries assigned to our mission, you can see that slightly less than half of the proselyting missionaries had cars. That sounds at first like a proselyting elder could plan on spending about half of his mission in a car.

However, there were other factors. Some areas were huge. They covered hundreds of square miles. It would have been a serious waste of time to have missionaries bike from appointment to appointment. Therefore, there were "car areas" in our mission. Some areas should have been car areas, but there were just not enough cars to go around. The elders rode bikes because it was the best we could do. It was always disheartening for us to see them biking twenty miles to an appointment when it was 110 degrees outside. They were troopers and seldom complained.

We thought it was inappropriate to have sisters riding bikes in their dresses. Even though several volunteered to take their turns on bikes, the weather, modesty, and safety all dictated that we put them in a car. Therefore, one car was taken for each pair of sisters. At times we had as many as thirty-two sisters—sixteen cars!

Many of the areas where languages were spoken overlapped English-speaking areas. One Spanish-speaking area may have covered five English-speaking areas. The same was true with the Southeast Asian language areas—they were huge. Therefore, it became necessary to put our language missionaries in cars as frequently as possible. You can begin to realize the headache for the mission president to try to meet the demands when there weren't more cars available. You might ask, "Why didn't the Church just give you more cars?" If you consider the worldwide expansion of the Church and the tremendous demands on Church resources to build chapels and temples, it seems reasonable that the Church would limit their automobile fleet as much as possible.

The final factor is where you come in. Each couple who flew to the mission field required one of the mission cars. There was never a question by the young missionaries that the couples should have a car—even if their area was considerably smaller than an area serviced by elders on bikes. Thankfully, parents had taught their sons well. We never had any hard feelings because we gave cars to the couples.

However, it was almost an event to cry over when we would talk to the couple and find that they could bring their own car. It freed one more car up to distribute on a priority basis to the young missionaries.

There is another factor you may not be familiar with. Each mission is allotted a certain number of miles per car. Thankfully, that limit is not placed on the mission president's car. Some of the missionaries had as few as 500 miles per month. Others who were serving in large areas had as many as 1,500 miles per month. Virtually every set of missionaries in a car felt they deserved more miles. They just weren't there to give.

This is where the couples were double lifesavers. First, they had their own cars, therefore not requiring a mission vehicle. Second, the Church did not impose a mileage limit on the couples' cars like they did the mission cars. Often at the end of the month we would find couples transporting younger missionaries to distant parts of their areas to conserve miles. We also noticed that when we held zone conferences near the end of the month, the couples always arrived with a car full of missionaries. When a couple had a van (which several did!) the missionaries would offer to pay them mileage to get them to zone conferences.

Now for the down side of couples having cars. Unless you have some pretty strict rules, the young missionaries would often start to take advantage of the good nature of the couples. They would play on their sympathy and try to make them feel guilty for not taking them to an appointment. Although it was usually done in good humor, we received several complaints that resulted in a reprimand being given to the elders who became too insistent in demanding rides. Just because you have your car there, and even if you don't have anything specifically planned for a certain block of time, you need not feel obligated to taxi the young missionaries around. Many couples chose to drive the younger missionaries around as it gave them time to talk with them and teach them where they seemed to need it.

More difficult than the young missionaries are the local people you will be serving. Many of them are totally dependent on public transportation. Although most major cities have good bus service, many of these shy people are reluctant to use them because their language is not fluent and they are afraid of getting lost. Unless we are sensitized to their plight, we might overlook the real reason they are reluctant to come to church on Sunday.

Should you give them rides to church, the store, the doctor, and so on? You need to be very aware of what your individual mission policy is. It requires that you adhere strictly to the insurance requirements. You may find that it is prohibitively expensive to carry enough insurance to legally transport your beloved people.

What seems like such a simple question has ramifications that boggle the mind. Our best advice is to call the mission president and discuss the matter with him. Take his advice, and if you feel comfortable taking your car with you to the mission field, the president certainly won't argue with you. The Church strongly encourages couples to drive to their mission in the United States and Canada.

There are two more factors to consider. First, you will be putting a lot of miles on your car while you are there. Unless you have means or have made provisions to replace your car when you return, you may find that you come home with a car that is worn out. This is not intended to say that you shouldn't take your car. It is only to make you aware so you can make arrangements. Your car is about the same as your life; you are willing to consecrate it to the building up of the kingdom knowing that someday both yourselves and your cars will expire.

The second consideration is the level of confidence you have driving in large cities. When we received our assignment to California, we had visions of freeways six lanes wide in each direction going a hundred miles an hour. In truth, if you are privileged to serve in Los Angeles, there will be freeways that are six lanes wide in each direction. However, they usually travel about ten or fifteen miles an hour!

If you have never driven in traffic before, it can be a little nerve racking. Virtually every one of our couples learned to drive safely around the city. Of course, Fresno isn't any Los Angeles either. Much of our mission was open road driving with little or no traffic. We are not aware of a single accident that involved our couples during their missions. We wish we could say the same of the younger missionaries. Don't let your fear of driving in big cities stop you from taking your car if that fear is based on the fact you have never driven in large cities before. You will be doing a lot of things in the next year to eighteen months that you have never done before.

If you do drive to the mission field, plan ahead. It will take extra time to get there. Allow plenty of travel time. It would be a tragedy to have a mission-ending accident while en route to the mission field. Even if you could make it in two or three long days, plan on three or four short days. You don't want to arrive so exhausted that it requires the first week for you to recover.

Your car, like yourselves, can be a blessing to your mission. Again, like yourselves, if you use wisdom and restraint, your car will make it to the end of your mission without major problems. If problems do occur with your car, there is usually a mechanic who is a member of the Church who can help you get it repaired as inexpensively as possible. Major repairs can put major stress on your budget because mission funds can't be used to repair private cars. As long as you are aware of all these factors, the decision is much easier to make. You will be traveling in the fast lane no matter whether you take your car or not. Be prepared for the ride of your life.

Chapter 11

WRITING AND CALLING HOME, VISITS FROM HOME

Perhaps you have sent sons or daughters on missions earlier in your married life. You know from your own experience how you looked forward to hearing from them. As a matter of fact, they were required by the "white bible" (missionary handbook) to write or email home weekly. Your letters and email communications will be no less enthusiastically received. Now instead of letters thrilling parents and siblings, the scope of your influence will include children, grandchildren, and sometimes great-grandchildren.

It is sort of hilarious how some children (and grandchildren) develop an overly protective attitude toward parents. They don't think you can survive without their constant watch care. To their total amazement, you actually do better in the mission field than you did with them hovering over you. It was not unusual for us to get calls from grown children trying to confirm that their parents were doing as well as their letters indicated. When we would assure them everything was going well, we almost wondered if they received our reassurances with the same skepticism. Did they then call the General Authorities to verify that everything was all right?

According to the location of your assigned field of labor, the young missionaries have strict restrictions put on them on the frequency with which they can call home. Email is the preferred means of communication. Couples are in an entirely different league. Frequent telephone conversations with children and grandchildren are permitted and encouraged. However, a strange thing happens. Often the couples become so engrossed in their work that they call less and less. When they do call, the conversations do not last very long. The thrill of talking with family members is secondary to the thrill of teaching the gospel to your beloved investigators and new members. It is difficult to describe, but it is evident to see.

For practical reasons, it is better to instruct your children to call you at a specified time and date. If they call when you are normally in your apartment, they are more likely to enjoy the opportunity to talk with you. If you have a large number of children and grandchildren who want to talk with you, it is easy to be on the phone over an hour. Then if they want to talk to your spouse, the time doubles. Many couples had two cell phones in their apartment so they didn't have to double the talk time. More recently, families use Zoom or some other platform so the entire family can communicate at the same time.

It is also a good idea to have the children coordinate their calling times so they are not frustrated by constantly getting your voice mail. Additionally, scheduling the times of their calls keeps the conversations from carrying on too long since you'll have to end one conversation before your next scheduled call is due. We don't want to make this into a huge issue, just one you need to take into account before you leave.

Although phone calls are wonderful, the most powerful, long-term impact comes from writing letters and emails. To hear your voice is reassuring that all is well. But the minute the call ends, they begin to forget what you said. A letter or email can be read and re-read time and again. Many times when adult children came to the mission field to drive home with their parents, they told us how much comfort and encouragement they had received from their folks' letters and emails. Time is allotted every week for the writing of letters and sending emails. If you are computer literate, it would be well to take a computer and printer with you. If you don't have one, you will surely have a member in the ward you are associated with who will be more than willing to let you use theirs.

With a computer you can change the name on your letter to be personalized and then add whatever counsel at the end is particular to that individual child. Even many of the couples who didn't use the computer when they arrived learned how to write letters on the computer to cut down the time it took to communicate with each child each week.

Don't plan on using the computers in the mission office for personal use unless you are assigned as an office couple. Those computers are kept going day and night to keep up with the business of running the mission.

We counseled the young missionaries to write their letters home on the same loose-leaf paper that they kept their journals on. The introduction of email makes it more difficult unless you never delete your "sent" mail. If you choose to keep a hard copy, then buy two journal covers before you leave. Leave one with a designated child and take the other with you. Then each week as you write home, they can file the letter in your journal binder at home. When you combine the journal you keep regularly in the mission field, the letters you send home reporting your mission to your children, and the president's letters you send weekly to the mission president that he will return to you at the end of your service, you have a very comprehensive record of your mission. Some senior missionaries assigned one child to print or make a file on their computer of all the emails sent during their mission. That way, nothing was lost.

Just a word of caution about writing home. At times things happen in the mission that sound really dangerous unless you were actually there. In fact, the news media are masters at making the most innocent events seem like national emergencies. If you are too graphic in describing some of the things that happen to you, you can bet the mission president will get a panicked call making sure you are all right. While we would never suggest that you be dishonest in what you write home, it may be wise to omit certain details until a while after the event is over.

If you talk too much about your sore knee or your bruised shoulder, your children are apt to read more into your letter than you intended. Emphasize the high points of your mission. Talk about the impact your teaching is having on your own and the lives of the people you are teaching. Write about the spiritual experiences you are having and the joy you are feeling from watching the gospel change people's lives. When you write to your grandsons, talk about *when* their mission time comes, not *if* they serve.

If you have the challenge of having one or more children or grandchildren who have temporarily lost their way in life, don't preach to them. Just write positive, inspirational letters and let the Lord take care of the rest. We have been witnesses to many miracles in the lives of children as a result of letters parents have written home.

Mention was made in a different chapter about visits to the mission field by family members. Perhaps a little more here would be appropriate. The most vital element on whether to have your children visit is the impact their visit will have on the work you are doing. You will discover almost from the first day you arrive that the amount of work you have to do is overwhelming. There seems to be so much to do and so little time available. Therefore, extended visits by family members would put undue pressure on you. While it is wonderful to see them, a day or two with a dozen grandchildren under foot and you are ready for them to leave.

Your mission president can help regulate the frequency and duration of the visits. Make sure you have his permission before inviting family members. You can always use him as the "heavy hand." Something as simple as "President said you are welcome to visit but may not stay for longer than two days." Few children care to tangle with the mission president. We used to receive calls almost weekly about family members wanting to visit their young missionaries in the field. Through experience we learned that a lengthy visit was often detrimental to the work and to the attitude of the missionary. We would allow them to take them and their companion out to dinner and stay a maximum of two hours. It worked well all the way around. We never had a family criticize the policy. After a couple of hours, many were ready to move on so their son or daughter could get back to the work that had become their life.

A picnic in the park is often more fun than trying to cram everyone into the apartment. Although your apartments will be adequate, they will not be spacious. Eating space, sleeping space, bathroom space, and even open space will be at a premium. If your family stays in a motel while they visit, you can direct them where to stay so you will have easy access to them and so they will be in a safe part of town.

We recommend you identify the most interesting two or three landmarks or tourist sites to see. Then keep them on the move during their visit. Remember, you must get permission from the mission president to go outside your assigned area. Even the mission president has to get permission before he can authorize your leaving the mission. The General Authorities are pretty busy to take time to authorize out-of-mission visits. Be considerate. Usually the mission president will be more than willing to authorize travel within the mission.

Although holidays are wonderful family times, they also pose some problems. If the planned visit is over the Christmas holiday, the weather is more likely to be a factor. It would be a tragedy of the first magnitude if your family was to be injured or killed traveling to or from a visit to you. Additionally, many members and investigators want to spend extra time with you during those special seasons. You can reduce the number of conflicts if you schedule their visits during a season other than Thanksgiving or Christmas. There is no rule that Christmas can't be celebrated in October or March just as well as in December. With a little creativity you can eliminate almost all conflicts so that your visits can be unhurried and enjoyable.

If you are serving a foreign mission, you may want to consider having your family come at the end of your service, then travel home together. Again, you will want to make arrangements through the mission president. He may have some guidelines that will minimize the conflicts with the mission. You must remember that the president has to send missionaries home, receive new missionaries, and conduct a major transfer in the mission all during the few days surrounding your departure. Be considerate of his time. Most mission presidents would love to be able to spend time with your family. We always felt like we short changed the families when they dropped in to see us around transfer time when our lives were so hectic.

If you plan to travel home with your families, have them check far in advance with Church Travel. If they will take the time, Church Travel can give you the information so you can book your family on the same flights and in adjacent seats. That seems much more desirable than flying home separately. You will have to plan your return in advance. If you plan to stay a few days so your family can see your field of labor, then tickets need to be arranged for in advance. These may seem like obvious items to consider, but our experience was that not all families took them into consideration.

You will remember that the mission president does not release missionaries—your local stake president does. Therefore, while you are traveling home, you are still on your mission. The rules are different for you than for the young missionaries. You are free to go sightseeing, to entertainment, to amusement parks, even swimming if you so desire. Just make sure you clear your proposed travel plans with your mission president and get his blessing.

Some couples used their mission experience to interest their older friends in serving missions. More than one couple came for a short visit, did missionary work with our senior couples, and returned home to submit their papers. Missionary work is infectious. It only takes one or two experiences to convince most couples that there is more to life than just watching the sun set.

You will soon discover that everything about a mission is calculated to increase your testimony, your love of the Lord, your appreciation of the Church, your faith in the Brethren, your love of life, and every other area of life that it touches. That is not only true for you as missionaries but it is equally true of those who share your mission with you through letters, emails, phone calls, and visits. Bless everyone you possibly can.

Chapter 12

WHAT IF PEOPLE ASK QUESTIONS WE CAN'T ANSWER?

One of the most frequently expressed fears of couples considering a mission is, "We don't know enough about the scriptures to answer difficult gospel questions!" For those of us who have been on missions, we realize that the fears are totally ungrounded. However, since so many consider that to be a real concern. Let us give you some ideas.

There are a couple of trains of logic that seem to focus the inquirer on the true source of answers to difficult questions. Especially if the person asking the questions seems to have obtained his questions from an anti-Mormon source, begin by saying, "If I can answer every one of your questions to your perfect satisfaction, does that automatically make the gospel that we are teaching you true?" The obvious answer is "no." Then ask, "If I can't answer any of your questions, but you do as James 1:5 instructs and 'ask of God,' and the Lord manifests you in an unmistakable way that the message is true, does the fact that I can't answer your questions mean the gospel is not true?" Again, the obvious answer is "no." The truthfulness of this gospel does not depend on you or me being able to answer their questions. It depends solely on whether the Lord manifests the truthfulness of the gospel to them.

I remember a time many years ago when I was discussing with a minister of another church about the claim that this is the only true church on the face of the whole earth (see D&C 1:30). He thought that was totally absurd and wanted to argue the point. In a flash of inspiration, I said, "If the Savior Himself appeared and told you that The Church of Jesus Christ of Latter-day Saints was the only true Church and He wanted you to join, would you?" He paused for a long time and then said, "No." I then continued: "If you wouldn't join even if the Savior asked you to, what chance do I have of convincing you the Church is true? I am wasting your time and mine!" With that we parted. Remember that it is the Lord who bore testimony that the Church is true, not just the members.

If you receive any flack at all from anti-Mormon sources, it will come from those who are not sincerely searching for the truth but those who are trying to show their intellectual superiority. Seldom will you be successful in convincing them of the error of their ways even if you have a doctor of theology degree. When your good, sincere investigators receive anti-Mormon literature from their minister, family, friends, or other well-intended but deceived people, you may have a greater degree of success if you use this simple logic: "If I wanted to know something about your church, would you think I would get good information if I talked to a minister of a different faith who was antagonistic? Would I get the true information if I talked to a person who had been excommunicated from your church because of heretical beliefs?" Both answers will be "no." "If I really want to know about your church, wouldn't it seem like the most reasonable approach to talk to someone who is a member and in good standing?" Any reasonable person will realize that you will get a tainted picture if you listen to apostates or those who have never been members.

Another tactic we like to use is having them compare how they feel when they read the anti-Mormon literature contrasted to the way they felt when you finished their last discussion or they read from the Book of Mormon. The feelings are on opposite ends of the continuum. Even though we have read considerable anti-literature, the ugly, dark, hollow feelings are still there every time we read them. Whenever you teach by the power of the Spirit, the people will feel uplifted, motivated, joyful, happy, filled. The reading of anti-Mormon literature will leave them empty and confused. The discussion of truth with you will leave them full of light and with increased understanding (see D&C 50:21–22).

Occasionally we will hear a would-be-investigator who does not understand say something like: "I took your challenge to read the Book of Mormon and the Lord told me it was not true!" If you have never encountered such an absurd statement, it may take you off guard. I generally say, "That is really interesting. Let me read you from Doctrine and Covenants 17:6, which says: 'And he [Joseph Smith] has translated the book, even that part which I have commanded him, and as your Lord and your God liveth it is true.' How do you account that the Lord solemnly testified to the entire world that the Book of Mormon is true and then you claim that He revealed to you that it is not true?" You are not called to convert—only to teach. The person responsible for the conversion of souls is the Holy Ghost. Don't try to magnify His calling.

Many of you have attended church meetings all of your lives. Even if you were not doctrinally or scripturally involved, you absorbed much more doctrine than you realize. As you continue to read and study the scriptures, the Lord made a wonderful promise: "Neither take ye thought beforehand what ye shall say; but treasure up in your minds continually the words of life, and it shall be given you in the very hour that portion that shall be meted unto every man" (D&C 84:85). If you will sincerely ask Heavenly Father to quicken your mind, it will happen.

Even as a young missionary, although I was not very well prepared scripturally, I received help with a difficult answer. We had been invited to visit a wonderful Samoan family who had consented to take the discussions. When we entered their fale (home), they nervously asked us to sit down on the mats on the floor. We started to teach them the first discussion. They were fidgety and continued looking outside like they were expecting some reinforcements. Before long four older men dressed in black lavalavas, white shirts, ties, and suit coats came in. They each had a Bible in their hands. We recognized them as the ministers of the local churches.

After the normal greeting, I explained that we were teaching the family and would be honored if they would participate. They agreed. Before I even finished the Joseph Smith story, the head minister raised his hand and demanded that I stop. He said they didn't believe what I was teaching and thought we were false ministers. However, he said they were all fair-minded men and if I could show them from their Bible where it said that "man would be punished for their own sins and not for Adam's transgression" all of the ministers, this family, and all of their congregations would join our church. He also warned that if we were unable to produce such a scripture, then they demanded that we leave since we were teaching false doctrine.

Does a scripture come to your mind that would answer his question? It didn't come to mine either. Just as I was ready to open my mouth and tell him we would have to search until we found one and return at a later time, I heard myself say: "Would you kindly turn to 2 Chronicles 25:4 and read it?" He smiled and looked at me as if to say, "Nice try kid, but nobody knows what is in 2 Chronicles 25:4!" In fact, I didn't know what was in that verse. He kept that condescending smile on his face as he leafed through the pages of his Bible. The smile disappeared as he read it to himself. He passed his Bible to the next minister, who read it and passed it to the third and fourth, in turn. They returned the Bible to the first minister. They were no longer smiling. They stood up and quickly departed. I hurriedly turned in my English Bible to 2 Chronicles 25:4 to see what it said. It reads: "But he slew not their children, but [did] as [it is] written in the law in the book of Moses, where the Lord commanded, saying, The fathers shall not die for the children, neither shall the children die for the fathers, but every man shall die for his own sin." I didn't have it marked then, but I do now. I have never forgotten that scripture since.

Just as a post script, the ministers didn't join the Church, neither did the family, nor their congregations. But two missionaries did! I have never since that time questioned that the Lord would fulfill His promise. Further in the Doctrine and Covenants the Lord promises: "Therefore, verily I say unto you, lift up your voices unto this people; speak the thoughts that I **shall** put into your hearts, and you shall not be confounded before men; For it **shall** be given you in the very hour, yea, **in the very moment**, what ye shall say. But a commandment I give unto you, that ye shall declare whatsoever thing ye declare in my name, in solemnity of heart, in the spirit of meekness, in all things. And I give unto you this promise, that inasmuch as ye do this the Holy Ghost shall be shed forth in bearing record unto all things whatsoever ye shall say" (D&C 100:5–8; emphasis added).

The experience I shared above is not a single occurrence. It was just the first and most dramatic that convinced me that the Lord really is in this work. Frequently, as a professional religion teacher, I have experienced the Lord bringing back to my mind, in the very moment, exactly the portion that every man needed. Let Him do the same for you. In all honesty, the larger problem for you will be the task of making the gospel so simple that your investigators cannot misunderstand. Note what the Lord said was the purpose and the simplicity of His gospel: "And for this cause, that men might be made partakers of the glories which were to be revealed, the Lord sent forth the fulness of his gospel, his everlasting covenant, reasoning in plainness and simplicity" (D&C 133:57).

The gospel is very logical. Remember that the Lord said to the early brethren: "And now come, saith the Lord, by the Spirit, unto the elders of his church, and let us reason together, that ye may understand; Let us reason even as a man reasoneth one with another face to face. Now, when a man reasoneth he is understood of man, because he reasoneth as a man; even so will I, the Lord, reason with you that you may understand" (D&C 50:10–12).

The same is true with us. When confronted with a question you are not sure about, ask yourself, "What is logical?" If you use good, solid logic, you will be correct most of the time. The only time the gospel is not logical is when our logic breaks down. The gospel is perfectly logical.

If your investigator is sincere, their questions will be clear and understandable. If they are looking for an argument, you will not be able to convince them anyway. Remember: "A fool convinced against his will, remains and unconvinced fool still." If the spirit of contention arises during your discussion, change the subject or postpone the discussion until another time. The spirit of contention is not of God (see 3 Nephi 11:28–29).

If your investigator is asking questions that will be answered later in the discussion, explain as much to them. "We'll be glad to cover that exact question during the next discussion." Most people realize that they can't learn the entire gospel in one setting. If they have received anti-Mormon literature, ask them if they would be willing to postpone your answering that question until after the discussion. As the Spirit of the Holy Ghost engulfs them during the discussion, you will find that they are really not interested in the answer to the foolish question by the time the discussion is over.

There is such a dramatic difference between the truth and error as taught in anti-Mormon literature that the honest, sincere seeker after truth can readily discern the difference. The Lord said: "And ye are called to bring to pass the gathering of mine elect; for mine elect hear my voice and harden not their hearts" (D&C 29:7). Those who are not at the present "elect" will not be taught by either you or an angel from heaven. The elect will not harden their hearts to the word so they will readily take instruction from you even if you don't have a doctorate degree from a theological college. There is such power in the simple truths of the gospel that every true seeker will find what you teach like cool water to their parched throats.

Put aside the fear of not knowing enough about the gospel. You are called by the Lord, and although we often fulfill His description of us, we are not called to fail. He said of His early missionaries in this dispensation, "Wherefore, I call upon the weak things of the world, those who are unlearned and despised, to thrash the nations by the power of my Spirit; And their arm shall be my arm, and I will be their shield and their buckler; and I will gird up their loins, and they shall fight manfully for me; and their enemies shall be under their feet; and I will let fall the sword in their behalf, and by the fire of mine indignation will I preserve them" (D&C 35:13–14).

The promise of thrashing the nations by the power of His Spirit is a sure promise. Great and marvelous works will be performed by those who are weak and unlearned. Why not be one of the ones through whom the Lord fulfills this promise?

Chapter 13

TEACHING INVESTIGATORS

One of the genuine surprises that most couples face is adjusting their level of teaching to match the knowledge and understanding of their investigators. A lifetime of sitting in Church meetings, listening to sermons, and learning and using Church jargon tend to make a couple more Church literate than you possibly believe.

At first you may wonder if you know enough to teach others the gospel. Within the first twenty-four hours of teaching, you will discover that unless you can greatly simplify your discussions, the people will likely never understand what you are talking about. One of the ways to simplify is to identify every word in your vocabulary that deals directly with the Church. For example, we talk freely about "meeting at the stake house" for a meeting. Seems understandable to us. To an investigator they can hardly see the logic of "meeting at a steak house" for a meeting! Acronyms like PEC, WCC, and PPI all mean something to us because of years of usage but are totally foreign to non-members and newly baptized members. In a state of total frustration, one investigator said, "I just can't understand you Mormons! You speak a totally foreign language." She was right. We are not as sensitive as we should be about our Mormonese!

Even after we define PEC as "priesthood executive committee meeting" or WCC as "ward correlation council," or PPI as "personal priesthood interview," they are still totally in the dark because they are not familiar with the terms. Taking the time to help them understand will seem like a waste of time to you. It would be like you walking through a nuclear science laboratory without being familiar with their terminology and wondering what in the world they were talking about. Lack of familiarity certainly does not indicate lack of intelligence.

After becoming more sensitive about the language peculiar to our church, you might consider how limited the understanding of the plan of salvation really is among the general population. They know nothing about a pre-earth life. They do call God "Heavenly Father," but very few, if any, have a concept that He is really our actual Father. None of them will know, understand, or believe that Jesus and Lucifer are brothers. That is so appalling to them that they consider it to be blasphemy. None of them will understand the war in heaven, although it is taught in the book of Revelation.

None of them will have a clearly stated purpose for earth life. Very few will really believe in personal revelation, although most will believe in prayer. Few will have deep understanding about the scriptures as the word of God, although most will profess to believe the scriptures. Almost all Christians will believe in baptism, but as to the mode, the authority necessary, and its essential nature, most of them will be totally clueless. None will understand the eternal nature of the marriage covenant, although some will claim to believe that they will be together as husband and wife forever. Absolutely none will have a concept of families being together forever.

Without the true understanding of mortality, many will unfairly criticize God for allowing such suffering among His children. Few will understand the essential nature of death to the plan of our Heavenly Father. Although virtually all Christians will believe in the Atonement, resurrection, and ascension of the resurrected Lord, none of them will have a very good understanding of these key doctrines.

Few, if any, will understand the event we call death. Their concept of where the spirit goes after the parting with our physical bodies is distorted to the point of being ludicrous. They understand little or nothing about the spirit world and who goes to each part. The Second Coming of the Savior is almost universally accepted among Christians but understood by few. They have a distorted view of being "quickened and caught up" at the Second Coming. They know nothing about the Millennium and the purpose thereof. They know little about the resurrection and the final judgment. They know even less about the conditions that will exist in the celestial, terrestrial, and telestial kingdoms and what people must do to qualify for each. They know absolutely nothing about the eternal destiny of man, which is to become like our Heavenly Father.

These are just a few of the doctrinal points that we take for granted that the world knows little or nothing about. They also do not believe in living prophets, although they greatly revere the dead ones. They know nothing, and many will not accept the Book of Mormon or any additional volumes of scriptures. One can just about point to any doctrine of the Church and see an area where the world is all but totally ignorant.

So, again, your teaching inadequacies will be more in the area of knowing too much rather than not knowing enough. If we were to list all of the doctrinal misunderstandings that non-members have, it would take many volumes. Perhaps the list given will be sufficient to demonstrate our point. If we accept the fact that our challenge is to teach simply enough to be understood, how are we to accomplish it?

You may take comfort that the Lord wants His gospel preached so people cannot misunderstand. He said:

> And for this cause, that men might be made partakers of the glories which were to be revealed, the Lord sent forth the fulness of his gospel, his everlasting covenant, **reasoning in plainness and simplicity**—
>
> To prepare the weak for those things which are coming on the earth, and for the Lord's errand in the day when the weak shall confound the wise, and the little one become a strong nation, and two shall put their tens of thousands to flight.
>
> And by the weak things of the earth the Lord shall thrash the nations by the power of his Spirit. (D&C 133:57–59, emphasis added)

Many of our senior couples went through the discussions and the new member discussions, then went back to their Primary books, pictures from the Distribution Center, old copies of the *New Era* and

Ensign magazines, and so forth to collect pictures they could put into a loose-leaf binder and use to supplement their discussions. It is veritably true that a single picture is worth more than a thousand words if you can display them artfully.

We make two major mistakes when teaching investigators. First, we try to teach too much; and second, we mistakenly believe that just hearing something once is sufficient to cause learning to occur. We will consider them in order.

First, we try to teach too much in one setting. If we watch the investigators closely, they will send silent messages when they are about to experience a spiritual overload. If you plan on taking about twice as long as you would normally think necessary to teach a concept, you will probably be right. When I was in Samoa, I was asked to substitute in Primary. Not having a regular manual, I decided to teach from the scriptures. In one forty-five-minute Primary lesson, I taught the entire Old Testament. Somehow, I don't think the children comprehended everything I taught.

Take the concepts slow and easy. It would be more effective if we would have the investigators teach a concept back to us after we have taught it to them. There isn't a much faster way of seeing how much they understand and where you need to re-teach the concepts more carefully. Sure it takes a long time to double teach (teaching it once to them and then the second time them teaching what you just taught back to you), but you are old enough to appreciate that all good things often take more time than you anticipated.

Too many young missionaries become frustrated when people have difficulty grasping these strange new concepts. Senior couples are generally much more patient and understanding. Perhaps that is one reason senior couples do such a remarkable job with the investigators the young missionaries have given up on as "impossible."

The second mistake we often make is believing that our investigators (or students) will comprehend and remember everything we teach them the first time they hear it. Countless hours of frustration would be saved if each missionary would set as a rule of thumb that a person must hear a concept between four and six times before it actually registers. Knowing that, wouldn't we be more productive in every teaching opportunity if we made sure the concepts were repeated several times? Consider reviewing your previous lesson before beginning the next lesson. One of the most effective ways of teaching a concept more than once, without giving the family the impression you think they are slow of mind, is to have them invite their friends into their home to hear the first discussion. You will have already given the first discussion to them. Now they hear it a second time as you present it to their close friends. If every family does that three or four times, you are well on your way to converting the host family. The others may also profit by having their friends in their homes for a first discussion.

In addition to the repetition, the host family has a vested interest in how well the discussion goes. No one wants to invite their good family friend over for a discussion that flops. Therefore, the host family tries a little harder to make sure their invited guests are understanding and having a good time. As you teach the friends of the host family, you may want to give the host family a chance to explain a concept in their own words. There isn't anything that converts like hearing yourself bear testimony of the truths of the gospel.

There is a possible downside to having either investigators or new members teach. Sometimes some of the wildest doctrine we have ever heard has been taught by overly enthused members. They want to go directly to what we call the "rafter doctrine." You builders know that the rafters are the last things to be put in place during the framing stage of building. So it is with certain doctrine. Seemingly the most favorite of the overly enthused are the concepts of the godship of man, Mother in Heaven, making one's calling and election sure, and so on. Although they may all be true doctrine, your investigators will not be equipped to comprehend such doctrine. Far better that you take it slow and easy and then let them teach each other and you.

It won't take you too long to identify those members who, in spite of repeated cautions and pleas, insist on teaching beyond the discussions. Wisdom would dictate that you find someone else to go with you to your appointments. Before long, the offending Saint begins to figure out why you don't call much. Then they have a serious choice to make: either curtail their comments or face the prospects of not going with the missionaries to teach.

From our experience in teaching investigators, we would suggest that you adopt a habit of watching carefully whoever in the family gives the best non-verbal feedback. We have found that generally the mother or the children are better at giving feedback than the husband or father. There seems to be this almost universal "macho" image that males try to keep. Even when they don't understand, they still give you that "poker face," which does not betray their lack of understanding. Often a woman or children will have puzzled looks on their faces, indicating that they are trying hard but just haven't be able to master the concept you are teaching.

It's far better to stay with that particular concept until they understand it rather than trying to put up the stud walls without a firm foundation to support them. As discussed previously, three things will always accompany you when you are teaching by the Spirit: (1) you will understand one another; (2) both will be edified; and (3) you will both rejoice together (see D&C 50:21–22). If you will look for understanding, you will soon discover in the body language of those you teach whether or not they are understanding you.

You are aware that there is an equal and opposite temptation for every blessing we receive. Brigham Young taught the concept powerfully when he said:

> I ask, is there a reason for men and women being exposed more constantly and more powerfully, to the power of the enemy, by having visions than by not having them? There is and it is simply this—God never bestows upon His people, or upon an individual, superior blessings without a severe trial to prove the , to prove that individual, or that people, to see whether they will keep their covenants with Him, and keep in remembrance what He has shown them. Then the greater the vision, the greater the display of the power of the enemy. And when such individuals are off their guard they are left to themselves, as Jesus was. For this express purpose the Father withdrew His spirit from His Son, at the time he was to be crucified. Jesus had been with his Father, talked with Him, dwelt in His bosom, and knew all about heaven, about making the earth, about the transgressions of man, and what would redeem the people, and that he was the character who was to redeem the

> sons of earth, and the earth itself from all sin that had come upon it. The light, knowledge, power, and glory with which he was clothed were far above or exceeded that of all others who had been upon the earth after the fall, consequently at the very moment, at the hour when the crisis come for him to off up his life, the Father withdrew Himself, withdrew His Spirit, and cast a vail over him. That is what made him sweat blood. If he had had the power of God upon him, he would not have sweat blood; but all was withdrawn from him, and a veil was cast over him, and he then plead with the Father not to forsake him. "No," says the Father, "you must have your trials, as well as others."
>
> So when individuals are blessed with visions, revelations, and great manifestations, look out, then the devil is nigh you, and you will be tempted in proportion to the vision, revelation, or manifestation you have received. Hence thousands, when they are off their guard, give way to the severe temptations which come upon them, and behold they are gone.[1]

Realizing that fact, it would be wise for you to take away the initiative of the adversary by explaining before you conclude the first discussion that they will probably experience some rather serious trials before your next meeting. If you fail to explain it to them, they may meet you at the door (or even worse, "dog you," which means not be there at the appointed time and place) and invite you to leave and never come back. If you have adequately warned them, they will more likely invite you in with open arms and excitedly tell you about the trials they have experienced since your last meeting.

Can you teach on a level your investigators will understand? Yes, if you can learn to teach simply enough. Practice now by teaching your grandchildren the discussions. If you can make the younger ones understand, you should do fine in the mission field.

NOTE

1. Brigham Young, *Journal of Discourses*, 3:205–6.

Chapter 14

KEEPING PACE WITH THE YOUNG MISSIONARIES—DON'T EVEN TRY!

The advantage of sending senior couples into the field is that they move at a slower pace and therefore make fewer mistakes. If you get the impression that you must match stride with the younger missionaries, you have missed your call. Some young missionaries run around at a frenzied pace because for them there seems to be no tomorrow. Therefore, they must do everything that can possibly be done today. Senior couples have ridden the earth around the sun enough times to realize that there was work to when you arrived, there will be plenty of work to do while you are here, and there will be even more work to do when you leave. If the Lord had planned it any other way, He would have had to send a lot more angelic help.

Both the scriptures and our modern-day leaders have made it clear that there is a limit on how far and how fast we are to move. The principle is not new. King Benjamin, during his final address to his beloved Saints many years before the birth of Christ, said: "And see that all these things are done in wisdom and order; for it is not requisite that a man should run faster than he has strength. And again, it is expedient that he should be diligent, that thereby he might win the prize; therefore, all things must be done in order" (Mosiah 4:27).

Perhaps realizing that our generation would live in the fast track, the Lord re-emphasized to Joseph Smith: "Do not run faster or labor more than you have strength and means provided to enable you to translate; but be diligent unto the end" (D&C 10:4). Although the Lord was specifically speaking to Joseph Smith about translating the plates, the general principle still applies to us today. It is more important to be diligent to the end than to burn ourselves out in a short burst of energy that is depleted before the end of our mission.

Through His latter-day leaders the Lord reaffirms the scriptural counsel:

> Many couples have concerns about leaving their homes and families, or they picture themselves being sent to a developing area of the world or struggling to learn a new language or trying to keep up with the younger missionaries' tracting and work pace. These concerns are generally unwarranted. Missionary couples are not expected to work at the same pace or follow the schedule of the younger missionaries. Mission presidents are sensitive to each couple's special need and establish activity and assignments that make the best use of abilities, experience, and talents.[1]

It would be unheard of that a mission president would make physical demands on a senior couple that would jeopardize their health. Elder Robert E. Wells puts a humorous twist on this area of rather grave concern. He said:

> Let me encourage you faithful married couples without children at home to go on missions. The Lord needs you out in the mission field. Forget your fears. We don't expect you to do everything the young missionaries do. In fact, I was in Idaho trying to eliminate the fears of some high priests, and I said, "You retired couples don't have to memorize scriptures like the young missionaries, you don't have to memorize any presentations unless you want to." I told them, "you don't have to get up early in the morning like the young missionaries do to study, and if it is raining or snowing, you don't have to go outside until you feel up to it. . . ." At that point a fellow down in the middle shot up his hand and said, "When can I go? That's a better life than I've got now!"[2]

Even though said in jest, the man was exactly right—mission life is a better life than you now have!

Of course, you will want to work to the limit of your abilities, but that doesn't mean you should feel bad about sleeping in occasionally to ward off a cold or the flu bug. Perhaps you can't stay out doing the work for twelve hours a day like the young missionaries. Most of our couples came back mid-afternoon for a power nap. The most challenging part for us as mission president was trying to get them to come in at a reasonable hour. They would become engrossed in what they were doing and forget to watch the time.

Every once in a while, you will get a young elder who has been called as a zone leader or a district leader who will not understand the difference between the senior couples and the other younger missionaries he is called to supervise. After a rather pointed confrontation with the senior couples about living the rules of the younger missionaries, I received a phone call from a senior sister. She explained their attempts to help him understand the different set of rules they lived by. The zone leader had become rather definite in his insistence that they would live by the same rules or else. This dear sister wanted to know how they should handle it.

I told her I would handle it for her. We called a meeting with the senior couples and the zone leader. Confident that he would be vindicated, the zone leader came in with a smirk on his face. After a few minutes of defining what was to be expected of the senior couples, I turned to the zone leader for his reaction. He immediately undertook his perceived duty to straighten me out. I listened patiently for a few minutes and then tried again to put the peculiar situation of the senior couples in perspective. Again, the zone leader took an argumentative stance. Finally, I said, "Elder, let me make it perfectly clear. If it comes down to you staying or the senior couples. You are history! Do you understand?" I think he got the message. Never again did any young elder order the senior couples around. It was a learning experience for him and a reinforcement for the couples. It was amazing how quickly that story circulated on the mission underground. Everyone knew how the president felt about senior couples.

If you need the backing of the mission president in order to help the young missionaries understand your limitations and rules, don't be afraid to ask. It is amazing how much weight a single word from the mission president carries!

Young missionaries are expected to spend the bulk of their time in proselyting activities. That may be different for senior couples depending on the needs of the mission. The mission president may have a variety of tasks that are mission related but don't specifically deal with proselyting that he would like you to focus on. Elder Jacob de Jager commented on this novel approach. He said: "We also have among the senior members of the Church retired office workers, bookkeepers, and even certified accountants. Couples with these qualifications may serve in the mission offices as mission secretaries, recorders, or financial secretaries. Moreover, there are among the mature couples those who have acquired a great expertise in genealogy and they can use their knowledge and experience, when specifically assigned to do so, to teach genealogical skills to members in wards and branches."[3]

Your talents will be used as they exist. You will develop new talents alongside the already existing ones. You will do things you were sure you would never be able to do. You will not be asked to do anything that you physically, emotionally, or mentally cannot do. Just because you cannot do exactly what the younger missionaries do, does not mean you are not vitally important to the missionary work. The ancient apostle Paul described it this way:

> For the body is not one member, but many. If the foot shall say, Because I am not the hand, I am not of the body; is it therefore not of the body? And if the ear shall say, Because I am not the eye, I am not of the body; is it therefore not of the body? If the whole body were an eye, where were the hearing? If the whole were hearing, where were the smelling? But now hath God set the members every one of them in the body, as it hath pleased him. And if they were all one member, where were the body? But now are they many members, yet but one body. And the eye cannot say unto the hand, I have no need of thee: nor again the head to the feet, I have no need of you. Nay, much more those members of the body, which seem to be more feeble, are necessary: And those members of the body, which we think to be less honourable, upon these we bestow more abundant honour; and our uncomely parts have more abundant comeliness. For our comely parts

> have no need: but God hath tempered the body together, having given more abundant honour to that part which lacked: That there should be no schism in the body; but that the members should have the same care one for another. And whether one member suffer, all the members suffer with it; or one member be honoured, all the members rejoice with it. Now ye are the body of Christ, and members in particular. (1 Corinthians 12:14–27)

Every member in the mission field must view himself or herself as a vital, indispensable part of the team. One is not more valuable than the other. The mission president has a certain role to fulfill. Without him and his wife, who would act as the head? Without the office staff, how would the logistical functions of the mission be performed? How would the referrals be distributed, the reports complied, and the records kept? Without assistants to the president, zone leaders, and district leaders, how would the mammoth task of administering the mission ever be accomplished? If it were not for the senior couples, how would the stability of the mission be maintained?

There is something to be said about working smarter rather than working harder. With some mature planning, senior couples often accomplished much more than did the young missionaries in much less time, with fewer miles and with much less expended energy. Planning your day wisely eliminates needless trips to distant parts of the area, thus wasting valuable time. Scheduling appointments to follow one another without huge gaps of time and without great distances between meetings saved gas, time, and money. You have been practicing working smarter all of your lives because you had to do that just to survive. Don't change a thing when you arrive in the mission field. You'll be a success just because you have been aware of the "work smarter, not harder" principle for many years.

It would be difficult to overestimate the value of senior couples. It would be equally as difficult to convince all the senior couples that they are no longer young missionaries and therefore need to slow down and be more reasonable about the pace they keep. Please know yourselves and be honest enough to realize when you need to take a break to allow your systems to catch up with your bodies.

Speaking from personal experience, we would rather have had a half a dozen couples who could only work at half speed than fifty younger missionaries who were like missiles out of control. Of course, once the younger missionaries learned some of the valuable lessons of life, they were as indispensable as the older couples. We love them all whether old or young. We were doubly grateful to have senior couples who knew themselves and didn't try to out run the younger missionaries.

NOTES

1. David B. Haight, *Ensign*, November 1988, 85.
2. Robert E. Wells, *Ensign*, November 1985, 27–28.
3. Jacob de Jager, *Ensign*, May 1981, 12.

Chapter 15

SENIORS' STABILIZING INFLUENCE ON YOUNG MISSIONARIES

Don't get the idea from the title of this chapter that you will be expected to "babysit" the young missionaries. That is definitely not the case. But there are some needs that you will automatically meet in your daily interfacing with the younger missionaries.

For many of the young missionaries, their mission is the first time they have been away from home. The accumulation of being separated from the familiar, the newness of their circumstances, and the total change of lifestyle from self-centered to other-centered often creates feelings of homesickness with which many missionaries are not prepared to cope. We have witnessed the powerful, calming influence of a single meeting with a senior couple on a struggling elder or sister. It doesn't seem to be so much what the couple does or says as much as their image reminding the struggling missionary of Grandpa and Grandma at home. A plate of homemade cookies, a dessert after a discussion, a dinner on Sunday afternoon, or just a friendly pat on the shoulders works miracles.

If the emotional dependency were to continue for a long period of time, it would be an unhealthy situation. But for the few days when homesickness is a serious problem, we see nothing but positive results. Often it requires mature insight to know when young missionaries are trying to establish an emotional tie that is not healthy. Other couples and the mission president will be able to help you determine when you are approaching that cautionary line.

Youth is often a time of impetuosity. When decisions involving the souls of the children of men are involved, time and patience need to be employed. Patience is not one of the long suits of this generation. A gentle reminder by a senior elder might help a young leader realize the potential impact of a rash decision. Recommending that a missionary be sent home for the least infraction was one area where we noticed a huge difference between those leaders who were interfacing with the senior couples and those who were not. The untutored were much more likely to suggest radical, drastic means to solve simple problems. Part of our task as mission president was to teach them not to react so emotionally to an affront to their authority. Senior couples greatly reduced our workload in this area.

This generation (probably not so different from when we were young) have not yet learned that everything is not a crisis. Very few things have to be decided right now. If we could help them to realize the power of the Lord's injunction to "be still and know that I am God" (D&C 101:16), we would have succeeded in helping them make great strides toward avoiding problems later in their mission and then in married life.

Although we did not use it very often, it was comforting to know that we could assign a missionary to a couple for a few of days to "cool off" if a serious breech occurred in a companionship. One elder would go with one couple and his companion with another. After a couple of days and some time to talk things through with the couples, the missionaries were able to get back together and resolve their differences. This also worked well with sisters who were prone to exaggerate their differences. What a stabilizing influence the couples were.

You may think the couples would resent being used as peacemakers, but we didn't find that to be the case. They really enjoyed having the young missionaries with them for a few days. If a couple ever expressed any hesitancy to the proposed arrangement, we immediately withdrew our offer. That only happened once or twice during our entire three-year mission.

We found the couples to have a delightful impact on the ZDMs (zone development meetings) and the DDMs (district development meetings) which were conducted weekly without the mission president. Often the senior sisters would bake cookies or a cake to take as a treat. That automatically made them the center of attention of the younger missionaries. More important than the food, the senior couples ensured that the meetings were conducted in a mature, orderly fashion. They didn't have to say a word. Just their presence prevented any childishness before it got started. Discussions stayed more in the main stream of the doctrine rather than on the fringes where some missionaries love to focus their attention. The meetings seldom went overtime. Missionaries returned to their own areas more quickly when senior couples were in attendance.

It is difficult to explain exactly why these things happened. Perhaps it was because the senior couples were more the age of the mission president and age does carry its image. The Prophet Joseph Smith complimented the seniors when he said, "I rejoice in hearing the testimony of my aged friends."[1] He further emphasized the importance of counseling with those who have experienced more of life by having lived a long time. "The way to get along in any important matter is to gather unto yourselves wise men, experienced and aged men, to assist in council in all times of trouble. Handsome men are not apt to be wise and strong-minded men; but the strength of a strong-minded man will generally create course features, like the rough, strong bough of the oak. You will always discover in the first glance of a man, in the outlines of his features something of his mind."[2]

So, in light of the Prophet's statement, those of you who have worried about not being too handsome, you can take courage. The weighty problems of life, the challenges you have to face, and the serious meditation you have engaged in all tend to make our features more coarse.

The next item shouldn't be, but it exists just the same. The younger generation sees the senior couples as less capable because many of us are physically impaired. Therefore, if the senior couples can tough it out, so can the younger missionaries.

Everyone in the mission knows the pace the mission president keeps. If he was not sustained daily by the Lord, he would collapse under the weight and the pace of his office. But he is supported. It was always amusing to listen quietly and empathetically to a young missionary explain to me how tired they were and how they just couldn't keep the pace. The amusing part came when they realized that they were talking to someone whose schedule made theirs look like a vacation.

Many times during interviews with the senior couples, we laughed together as they recounted similar experiences in their conversations with the younger missionaries. Some of our couples had to hobble along because of arthritic conditions. Others were somewhat lame because of accidents earlier in life. They didn't bound up the stairs, they didn't play basketball, they didn't run to the car or anywhere else—but they were steady. Often the young missionaries would comment how amazed they were at the strength and stamina of the older couples. I was not offended when they would include me in their categorization of "older couples," even though I was still in my forties!

Hopefully, the next item will never happen, but if it does it is just one more area where couples provide valuable learning situations for the younger missionaries. Occasionally one of our senior elders or sisters would become ill. When the word got out to the rest of the zone, one would think the world had come to an end. Flowers, get-well cards, anxious visits, even meals cooked by the elders would arrive. Zone prayers were held, help was offered, and calls were made to the mission office to make sure the president knew of the problem. It was nothing short of miraculous to see the Christ-like concern the elders and sisters had when a senior went down. The irony is that the same degree of concern was lacking when one of their own went down.

We are not suggesting that you get sick just to help them learn a lesson, but if it should happen, you will likely be treated to a faith-building experience. Don't resist their offers to help. One of the tactics inspired by Satan and strangling our entire generation is the focus inward. Let them sense the joy that comes from inconveniencing themselves, in addition to their heavy workload, in taking care of you.

If you happen to be in a mission where several couples are serving, you will soon discover that they become some of your very best friends. We had to watch our couples a little. They sort of became "party animals." Not really, but we used to tease them all the time. They would eat out together, have home evening together, and get together at the end of the day for ice cream and to share the experiences of the day. If we couldn't locate a certain couple in the late evenings, we often could call another couple's apartment and find the whole group gathered, having a wonderful time. They acted almost like children at times when they would try to get everyone to be quiet so the president wouldn't find out they were all together again! We loved our couples and laughed a lot with them. We also ate out with them more than we should have. It was always fun to go to the local buffet. It was the only time my wife and I were offered the senior citizen discount!

On a more serious and sober note. Many (far too many!) of the young missionaries came from less than ideal homes. Divorce, fighting and bickering, single parent homes, you name it—we had missionaries from those kinds of backgrounds. Likely the senior couples will never know that the example they set of an "old couple" still happily in love restored the broken confidence of the young missionary in the viability of marriage.

When Sister Bott asked what the missionaries would remember most about what I had taught the mission, she was surprised to hear them say that they loved and learned more about mature love by watching us walk hand in hand to the zone conferences. Don't underestimate the influence your example has on an often-disillusioned raising generation.

Those days spent with the couples will never be forgotten. Even we felt comforted when the senior couples were around. It was a sad day for everyone, especially the young missionaries, when a senior couple came to the end of their mission. Tears flowed freely from not only the local people but also from the missionaries when the goodbyes were said. Promises to keep in touch were made, and home addresses were exchanged. Many of the senior couples reported that it was as difficult leaving the young missionaries as it had been leaving their own families.

Many of the younger missionaries would weep openly during their exit interviews as they bore thankful testimony about the major impact the senior couples had had upon their lives and their missions. I only wished I could have had the senior couples sitting in the room with me when those expressions of love and thankfulness were expressed. Often young people are reluctant to express how they really feel because it doesn't fit into that macho image they would like to portray.

When a young missionary would leave the mission at the conclusion of their assigned time, there was always another to take his or her place. Therefore, the work went on as though they had never been there. That isn't the case with the senior couples. Although another couple often came to work with the same people, no one ever took the place of the couple. They were missed, talked about, plead with to return, and revered because of the priceless work they had done.

At our mission reunions, the couples were often the center of attention. Their powerful impact continued as they were invited to weddings, received birth announcements, and were visited by missionaries as they found their eternal companions. Our couples still get together regularly for a trip to the local buffet. We are graciously invited and make it as often as our schedules permit. What more can we say? The success of our time as mission president was in large measure due to the influence of the senior missionaries on everyone they touched—including the mission president and his wife. God bless forever our senior couples.

NOTES

1. *Teachings of the Prophet Joseph Smith,* 361.
2. Ibid., 299.

Chapter 16

HELPING STRUGGLING WARDS AND BRANCHES

One of the greatest faults we see regarding senior couples is their unwillingness to recognize the tremendous talents they have. While it may be true that your lot in life has not been to sit up front and conduct the meetings, it is not true that you don't have a vast amount of experience that is desperately needed in the mission field.

Many times we received phone calls from priesthood leaders pleading with us to send them a couple. What a difficult decision for a mission president to tell one branch they couldn't have their requested couple while an adjacent branch joyfully received the news that a couple had been assigned to their branch. There just wasn't enough—near enough—couples to fill the demand.

So, what kind of work do you do with the branches and wards? Much of what you do will be under the direction of the unit leadership. If the branch president wants you to visit the less actives, then that is what you will do. Some of these good people moved from their original home where they had joined the Church and were very active but just didn't bother to re-establish ties when they arrived at their new residence. Many times a single visit from a senior couple resulted in full activity in the Church. Many of the bishops and branch presidents serving in our mission had at one time been less active, but through the loving persistence of a home teacher or visiting teacher, they were reactivated and now led the local unit.

Can you imagine having five hundred names of less-than-active members to visit? That is not uncommon in many areas. Normal home and visiting teachers (now ministering brothers and sisters) cannot catch up with these good people because their schedules are such that they just don't have the time. You have the time and the tenacity to keep trying until contact is made. Just letting people know you are there and that you care about their well-being can work miracles. Letting them know they are needed and missed gives purpose to their lives. Knowing that they have a friend to sit with when they make their first visit back to the Church allays many fears.

We have heard of a single couple who reactivated hundreds during their brief mission. Elder Dallin H. Oaks said: "Our older couple missionaries, now numbering over 2,600 throughout the world, provide an unequaled example of Christian service. Who could calculate the contribution these couples are making in furthering the mission of the Church? They preach the gospel, strengthen leaders and members in struggling branches, serve in temples and visitors' centers, and in countless other ways accomplish the essential work of the kingdom, both the important and the routine."[1]

According to the location of your assigned field of labor, you may be instrumental in getting dozens of families prepared to be sealed in the temples. What a thrill to be able to go with them and watch that sacred ordinance performed that binds them together forever. Even if your mission does not have a temple nearby, the prospects of you preparing people to make the trip to a temple creates visions of celestial beings all eternally grateful to you for your efforts.

In addition to the temple blessings, senior couples can have a great impact on the quality of home and family lives. Without the gospel to make sense out of life, many people become discouraged and quit. Divorce is rampant and so terribly destructive to many families both inside and outside the Church. Without weekly contact with the saving truths of the gospel, people often slip into habits that are destructive to continued family life. Abuse occurs between spouses and with children. Relationships are weakened, confidences destroyed, and lives ruined because people have forgotten that the gospel, when applied, is the Lord's "message of peace" to us (see D&C 88, heading).

You may not be professional counselors, but the fact that you are still married after all these years makes you a rare commodity. Millions of marriage counselors "tell us how to do it" every day and then return to their own broken homes in the evening. You are likely very different. Life may not have been easy for you either, but you have weathered the storms and are now in a position to help others get a better "fix" on their eternal destination. Just offering advice that has worked for you may trigger ideas that will help the struggling Saints find their way out of the maze they have become entangled in.

Having lived long enough and watched enough couples struggle through the hard times, you are in a position to help people see that there may be many choices to help them cope with their problems. Maybe you haven't experienced the same problems the family you are working with has, but you may know of someone who has. That's what qualifies you as an expert.

If there is abuse occurring in the family, you are in a better place than the bishop or branch president to report it. You are not under the Priest/Penitent Privilege, which requires confidentiality. You can counsel with your mission president or the local priesthood leaders in individual cases so you will not make a mistake. There is even a hot-line set up for priesthood leaders in Salt Lake City to give them direction on how to cope with these ugly problems. Hopefully, you will not become entangled in too many of those experiences. In case you are, you can turn to your leaders for help when the situation goes beyond your level of expertise.

Many of the routine tasks performed every Sunday are novel and frightening to the new leader. How to conduct music, how to pass the sacrament, how to give a talk, how to prepare a lesson, how to delegate assignments, how to conduct a meeting—the list is endless. Even without professional training, your years of Church activity have allowed you to witness people who seemed expert in those things and those who were still learning. With a little effort you can identify the difference between proficiency and needing practice. A little one-on-one time with a willing but frightened convert can help them stand with confidence as they lead the music in Primary.

You may not have been trained as a professional teacher. No matter. You have listened to enough lessons, both dynamic and slow, to know what makes for a good lesson. You may not know the scriptures as well as you'd like, but you have had enough experience over the years to recognize when the Spirit is raising a warning flag about certain doctrine that is being taught. You may not have had a position that required that you conduct sacrament meeting or Relief Society, but you have witnessed thousands of times when people have.

Just as an experiment, we asked our missionaries to outline a sacrament meeting for us. Each wrote down the sequence they thought the meeting was to take. Other than an occasional juxta-positioning of the announcements and the ward business, they unanimously ordered the meetings the same. We would suspect that the Lord would not reject the sacrament meeting that gave the announcements after the opening song and prayer.

While it may be true that neither of you have served as the ward family history specialist, it does not then follow that you know nothing about records. In many struggling branches the records are so mixed up that it will take someone like you with a little know how, a lot of time, and even more love to help them get things straightened out. We watched order come from chaos many times as our senior couples would work through the records with the branch membership clerk. We also witnessed the tears of gratitude when our unpretentious couples helped a struggling branch president get control of all of the organizations in the branch that seemed so far beyond his administrative ability.

Your ability to conquer challenges one at a time cannot be duplicated by the young missionaries who have neither the time nor the patience to perform these vital functions. Recognizing a need and taking the initiative to help the enthused but untrained Saints succeed will require more time than you have.

Likely, when you arrive in your assigned area of labor, no one will be there to define your workload. It will be up to you to watch how things are being done and then ease into your helping role. Some leaders will gladly receive your help. Others may be more reluctant until they see for themselves the progress being made by those who have accepted your help. It was fun to watch the softening of the proud leader who didn't need any help as the senior couples loved their way into the hearts of the more teachable. We can't remember a time when even the proud didn't finally humble themselves and ask for help.

You may end up splitting up to do ministering assignments. The sisters in the branch can learn so much from your quiet example of what it means to visit in the home and leave a message of hope and inspiration. The men of the branch can catch the vision of what it means to shepherd a family in all ways—temporal, spiritual, emotional, and intellectual. Ministering sounds so simple unless you have never had ministers in your home or unless you have never done ministering yourself. Your years of faithful service cannot be duplicated by all the enthusiasm in the world. You can develop an army of ministering brothers and sisters who will assume their rightful roles and free more of your time to be able to move on to other areas of need.

You will likely sit in on branch administrative meetings, presidency meetings, and planning meetings. Although you will not be the leaders, your guidance and advice will be greatly appreciated. You will need to exercise some restraint and caution. Your word or opinion will become law. Unless you are very careful, the leaders will begin to look to you for everything. If you remember that your role is to teach them to be self-sufficient, then you can reflect back their responsibility to make the decisions. The same is true in the priesthood, Relief Society, and Sunday School classes you attend. Be sure you don't become the authority on every subject. It will require some restraint on your part not to right every wrong, fix every leak, and jump in to save every struggling leader.

If they become totally dependent on you, then chaos will again reign when you leave. Remember, you are trying to work yourselves out of a job. Teach them to be so proficient that they can easily do without you. You needn't worry if you are totally successful and one branch becomes celestialized—there are many more who need your help. Our work will never be done before the Millennium.

You may have sensed already that we could look carefully at each and every phase of Church administration and identify a place where you would be needed. That is exactly correct. This chapter could be easily enlarged to be an entire book. Our purpose is merely to introduce enough ideas that will act as catalysts to get you thinking about how much you have to offer. We have not seen a couple yet who felt they had nothing to contribute—after they had been in the branch a few weeks.

So when you arrive, begin immediately to define your own job description. If there is an area that you feel totally unprepared to assist in, don't worry. There will be a thousand other areas where you might be more comfortable. You will never be able to meet all of the needs of the people even if you are totally competent in all areas.

Leadership positions in your earlier lives can be very helpful. They can also be detrimental. Sometimes, having served, we develop the attitude that our way is the only way something can be done. For those who have served in leadership positions, hopefully you are willing to admit that not everyone has exactly the same talents and aptitude you have. Allow for individual differences. If a leader chooses to try a new, different approach, don't condemn. Surprisingly, many of the most effective leadership styles have been introduced by new converts. Many of our couples marveled at how they wished they had been able to lead as effectively after fifty years of Church service as a new branch president was after just a couple of years. The Lord is in this work. He is the one who raises leaders up and moves the great cause of Zion forward. We should be honored to be part of His marvelous plan.

So, do you have anything to contribute? Without fear of rebuttal, the answer is a resounding "YES." The only thing necessary is for you to fill out your papers and gain your personal testimony that what we are saying is absolutely true. Let the Lord bring out the leadership traits in your personality which, living in a large ward with multitudes of capable people, may not have been developed earlier in your lives. We saw so many couples blossom in the field.

Dirt farmers became almost like polished statesmen. Homemakers resembled congresswomen and prime ministers. Surely their families must have marveled as they returned home entirely different than when they left. The miracle is not restricted to the "born again" transformation that takes place in the lives of the people you teach. The miracle is yours. The cost of the miracle is your willingness to accept the call to serve. Put the Lord to the test and watch the miracle happen.

NOTE

1. Dallin H. Oaks, *Ensign*, November 1989, 64.

Chapter 17

WHAT IF ONE OF US GETS SICK WHILE SERVING?

One of the fears often voiced by those who are considering serving is the fear of getting sick while away on a mission. Although it is always a possibility, it is also a good possibility that you will get sick when you are at home. You may say, "At least at home we have family to watch out for us." In chapter 15 we mentioned the therapeutic effect that allowing the younger missionaries to serve senior couples had on them. There are other blessings that you should be aware of that have been promised by the Lord.

Speaking of those who were going on missions, the Lord said: "And any man that shall go and preach this gospel of the kingdom, and fail not to continue faithful in all things, shall not be weary in mind, neither darkened, neither in body, limb, nor joint; and a hair of his head shall not fall to the ground unnoticed. And they shall not go hungry, neither athirst" (D&C 84:80). We have been firsthand witnesses to the fulfillment of the Lord's promise, both in our own lives and the lives of our missionaries. As mission president, I did not see how I could go twenty-four hours a day, seven days a week, for three years without ruining my health. During the entire three years we served, I never experienced one sick day! There were days when I had a cold or a headache, but never a day I couldn't perform the duties that were mine. The same is true of my wife.

You might say, "Well, you were the mission president. You were different from the couples." The miracle of miracles would occur when the senior couples would arrive. During the initial interview, we would ask them about their health. Frequently, they would recite a list of health problems one or both had experienced. Our counsel to them was to guard their health and not try to run faster nor labor more than their physical stamina would allow. We gave them the latitude of going to bed when their bodies dictated that they were exhausted, rising when they felt they had enough rest, taking a nap during the day if necessary, and modifying their work schedule in whatever way was necessary so they felt physically well.

Some of the couples were pretty beat up physically when they arrived. We watched them with great concern for the first few months. As the couples settled into their labors, the miracle began. They started getting up earlier and staying up later. Their needed naps during the day were either greatly reduced or eliminated all together. Then we started to worry on the other end. They were getting up too early and staying up too late. As we counseled with them, they often said they had never felt this much energy in their entire lives.

The young missionaries used to marvel that the "old couples" could keep such a pace. Our greatest concern was that the couples, recognizing the limitless need that faced them, would try to work too hard and therefore ruin their health. Our fears were ungrounded. The Lord really did sustain the senior couples.

Occasionally one or the other would get sick. With the young missionaries, there was always a little tension when one would get ill. The other wanted to get out and work and since they had been assigned by the mission president to work with each other, sometimes their love for and devotion to each other was still in the developmental stages. This is not the case with couples. You have a great interest and concern for each other. If one gets sick, the other becomes very concerned and is willing to make whatever sacrifices are necessary in their personal schedule to ensure the healing and comfort of the other.

Generally, other senior couples are also very concerned if you become ill. There are always ward and branch members who hover over the couples like they are a fine piece of china, so fragile that the least bump might break it. Very often, rather than feeling isolated because you are away from family, you will feel the opposite. "Oh, if we could just have a little quiet and not so many visitors!" "We will never be able to eat all of the food the Saints have brought in for us!" These are just representative statements made by couples when they stayed home one day because of a cold or flu-like symptoms.

If you do become ill or injured, there are medical facilities in the mission field just like there are at home. Many times the medical help available is better than what you had at home. Doctors, many of whom are Latter-day Saints (but many are not), are very concerned that you stay in good health. We enjoyed the luxury of having doctors make house calls to many of our senior couples—just to check up on them and make sure they were not hiding any serious illnesses. Prescription drugs were available and again, often hand delivered.

Your local insurance should cover you no matter where you serve. Medicare and Medicaid also cover you in case of an illness. No mission is so large that the mission president and his wife cannot visit you or even invite you to come and stay with them in the mission home. Fear of sickness should not be a reason for declining a mission call. Put the Lord to the test and see if He will fulfill His promise.

The far more prevalent problem senior missionaries face, which is also faced by younger missionaries, is the mental fluctuations or mood swings. Every emotion is greatly intensified in the mission field. The "highs" you will experience will be higher than anything you have ever experienced. The "lows" will be lower than you can imagine. The difficulty is the frequency with which many missionaries experience the mood swings. If you understand the cause, then the control is much easier. Perhaps a couple of scriptures with some explanation will clarify the issue. The Lord explained: "And it must needs be that the devil should tempt the children of men, or they could not be agents unto themselves; for if they never should have bitter they could not know the sweet" (D&C 29:39). It appears that the devil plays a rather vital role in the mortal experience for the children of men. However, as the Lord warns the Saints about their relationship to the adversary, there is an entirely different role: "And while we were yet in the Spirit, the Lord commanded us that we should write the vision; for we beheld Satan, that old serpent, even the devil, who rebelled against God, and sought to take the kingdom of our God and his Christ—Wherefore, he maketh war with the saints of God, and encompasseth them round about" (D&C 76:28–29).

Did you notice the difference in intensity? He "tempts" the children of men (non-members), but he maketh "war" with the Saints of God. Since you fall into the latter category, the Lord also explains Satan's tactics. He said that the devil "encompasseth them round about." Encompass means to completely and totally surround. Then it would be less than wise if the Lord's "Saints" didn't realize that there is not a part of their lives that will not be subject to the attacks from the adversary. Because you pose such a threat to the adversary's kingdom, he will do everything in his devilish power to neutralize your effectiveness as a missionary. Thankfully, the Lord has revealed: "Verily, thus saith the Lord unto you—there is no weapon that is formed against you shall prosper" (D&C 71:9).

If you do not realize what is happening to you, it is very easy for the adversary to hit you from a position where you least expect it. As missionaries, you should keep your guard up in all areas. Your relationship with each other will be tested more than at any other time. Your confidence in your own ability to do what the Lord has called you to do will be challenged. Your physical stamina will be contested but not to the point of compromising your health. You may wonder if your memory is failing you, your ability to express yourself is sufficient, your personality lends itself to the work, your understanding of life and its challenges is deep enough, and so on. The adversary wouldn't be a very good devil unless he "encompassed" us round about.

Hopefully, over the years you have developed a strategy for coping with mood swings. It may require that you take a little time off to find a park and go for a walk. Joseph Smith had a Sacred Grove to resort to in times of real confusion. The Savior had a Garden He resorted to when He was deeply troubled. Why should you and I be any different? It may only take a few minutes to get life back into proper perspective. Don't wait until you are battling major depression before you stop and collect yourselves.

Because perfection is the goal of every Latter-day Saint who understands the plan of salvation of our Heavenly Father, it is easy to get down on ourselves when we see how far we have to go before we achieve our eternal goal. However, one of the tactics Satan uses in attempting to destroy us is to tempt us to engage in negative self-talk. When you look in the mirror and all you see is how ugly you are, or how many wrinkles you have, or how far you fall short of your potential, or how everyone else has their act totally together and you don't, or all of the other negative things we tell ourselves, then we play into the devil's hands. Since our Heavenly Father is all powerful, He could literally mend our infirmities in an instant and still have sufficient power to control the universe. The fact that He has chosen not to repair all our shortcomings would indicate that there is divine purpose in those weaknesses. In fact there is!

Many hundreds of years ago, the Savior told Moroni: "And if men come unto me I will show unto them their weakness. I give unto men weakness that they may be humble; and my grace is sufficient for all men that humble themselves before me; for if they humble themselves before me, and have faith in me, **then will I make weak things become strong unto them**" (Ether 12:27; emphasis added). The very "weaknesses" we see in ourselves, the Lord promises to turn into our strengths if we will be humble enough to look to him for help.

As we struggle to stabilize our world, perhaps counting our many blessings would bear some immediate fruit. In just a few short minutes, by focusing on all that we have and all that the Lord has done for us, we can overcome Satan's best efforts at discouraging us. It seems to be an eternal truth that we see and get in life exactly what we look for and expect. The Lord said: "Verily, verily, I say unto you, even as you desire of me so it shall be unto you; and if you desire, you shall be the means of doing much good in this generation" (D&C 6:8). Wouldn't it be a terrible disappointment if we arrived in the spirit world and discovered that we got exactly what we wanted out of life? Why not expect the best—then we won't be disappointed?

Perhaps re-reading together your patriarchal blessings would reassure you both that you are highly favored of the Lord and that He has work for you both to do. You might also consider getting a priesthood blessing of comfort from the mission president or from an elder in the mission. Some of the most revelatory blessings we have ever heard have come at the request of the senior couples.

If you discover that depressing feelings continue to linger beyond a reasonable time (never longer than a week), then call the mission president and get some help. Sometimes we get so close to the situation that we fail to see the obvious solution. Someone who has a priesthood stewardship over you standing a little farther away can give insight that is so obvious when we hear it that we wonder why we didn't see it ourselves. Some suffering seems to be good for the soul. When it is avoidable, we would be foolish not to take advantage of the escape.

If the unthinkable should happen (one of you dies in the mission field), what would you do? It seldom happens, but at our age, anything is possible. First, we should be comforted in knowing that we couldn't be doing anything better with our time. The Lord so stated: "And now, behold, I say unto you, that the thing which will be of the most worth unto you will be to declare repentance unto this people, that you may bring souls unto me, that you may rest with them in the kingdom of my Father" (D&C 15:6).

Second, we should know that our foreordained departure time was here. The Lord told the imprisoned Prophet, "For there is a time appointed for every man, according as his works shall be" (D&C 121:25). Further in the same revelatory letter, the Lord continued to comfort Joseph by saying, "Therefore, hold on thy way, and the priesthood shall remain with thee; for their bounds are set, they cannot pass. Thy days are known, and thy years shall not be numbered less; therefore, fear not what man can do, for God shall be with you forever and ever" (D&C 122:9).

Third, the very thing we have been working for (eternal life) is the promised reward for dying in His service. The Lord said, "And whoso layeth down his life in my cause, for my name's sake, shall find it again, even life eternal" (D&C 98:13). With those promises, why should we be unduly concerned about what happens to us?

If something should happen to either of you, rest assured that the Church would make all of the arrangements necessary to get you both home and cared for. You will have a mission president who will hover over you like your own children do. Your needs will be met, and you will find that the Lord really does watch out for His special servants. Put aside health concerns. The Lord is in control, and He will never let anything happen to either of you that would be to your eternal detriment. If you are a typical senior couple, you will stand and bear witness that the Lord increased your health and strength many times over while you are in his full-time service. Had we not been eyewitnesses to that very fact, we would not be so bold in making the promise to you.

Chapter 18

MULTIPLE MISSIONS

You may be saying, "Hold on! We haven't even decided for sure that we will go on our first couple mission yet!" We just want to warn you that missions are addictive. Just decide to go on a single mission to begin with. That will satisfy the Lord's requirements given through His servants. Enjoy your first mission with the idea in mind that after it is over you will come home and put your feet up and enjoy the remainder of your mortal days. Make plans for the rest of your life after your mission. You may even make promises to your children that this is a one-time event.

You may do all of those things, but be prepared to humbly admit that your vision of the future was not as full and complete as the Lord's. President Russell M. Nelson has lived long enough and traveled the world enough times to see both the need and the couples who are serving. He said: "There are pioneers in the Church today just as strong and courageous. Recently, I interviewed a married couple three days after their release as full-time missionaries in a large metropolis. 'We are converts,' they said. 'We joined the Church ten years ago. Even though we just completed a mission, we want to go again! But this time, we would like to volunteer for a more difficult assignment. We want to teach and serve children of God who live in remote areas of the world!'"[1]

We are unable to identify exactly what gets into the blood of the senior couples that would cause them to consider leaving their beloved families for yet another year or eighteen months. Even though it isn't readily identifiable, it is definitely real. We had couples serving with us who were on their second, third, fourth, and even fifth missions. Didn't they love their families? Of course they did. Their apartments were cluttered with pictures of children and grandchildren. The walls had to be refinished when they left because of the number of holes they had punched in them to hang family portraits, special pictures, pictures from grandchildren, and counted cross-stitch sayings from family members. But they claimed that it was because of their tremendous love for their families that they had decided to serve again.

President Gordon B. Hinckley also encountered some of these hearty, modern-day pioneers. He said:

> He and his wife are there, with others of their kind. They are two of a band of remarkable and dedicated older missionary couples who minister to the wants of people with numerous problems. They receive no financial compensation. They pay their own way. This world's goods mean little to them. As I said, they sold all they had when they left to come to the Philippines. They will stay for as long as they are assigned by the Church to do so. Then they want to go on another mission. They are healers among the people, serving in the cause of the Master Healer.[2]

Perhaps that is what it is all about. The more Christ-like we become, the more we are unable to sit at home enjoying the comforts of life, realizing that there are millions, even billions, of our brothers and sisters out there who need our help so badly. Until we experience firsthand some of the needs that we are talking about, we give lip service that they exist, but in our hearts we have not yet realized their importance.

Assuming that you will discover what we are talking about when you immerse yourselves in your first mission, let's consider some options. Many couples may not realize that you may extend, with the permission of the mission president, beyond the time of your original call. A phone call by the mission president to the missionary committee of the Church is all that is required. We have not witnessed any resistance on the part of the Church to accept your request. We did have one couple who wanted to return home for a couple of weeks to put their affairs in order before resuming their mission. Perhaps it was because our mission was so close to Utah that the permission was readily given. If you were a great distance away, perhaps returning home for a short time may not be as financially feasible.

We found that couples who were considering another mission could request where they wanted to serve. Although they may be assigned some other place, often their request was honored. From our own experience while serving as mission president, we learned that if we recruited couples, we could also request them to serve with us. Only once did we recruit and request but the couple was sent elsewhere. They were very pleased with their assignment, so it wasn't like the world came to an end.

You should be aware that if a couple wants to go to a mission outside the United States, they would normally be expected to sign up for eighteen months or two years. If a year is as long as you feel you can serve, you will likely be assigned within the United States or Canada. There are both advantages and disadvantages in serving locally and abroad. Many local missions need your help as badly as do the foreign ones. You are closer to home, medical facilities are generally good, and visits from family members are generally more feasible. Serving foreign missions often requires a foreign language, relying upon public transportation, adjusting to strange cultures and customs, and getting used to strange and exotic foods. However, seeing a new part of the world often changes one's entire outlook on the brotherhood of mankind. Once you see that skin color is only superficial, you will likely develop a deeper love and respect for our brothers and sisters no matter where they live. Serving in a strange land, although often challenging, is doubly rewarding. The help you give, although seemingly minor to you, is received with such thankfulness that you can't help but feel a satisfaction that comes in no other way.

It really isn't so much where you serve that makes the difference. Many of our couples who were on their multiple missions liked to mix foreign with stateside—for example, a mission to Australia was followed by a mission to California. There are also a variety of missions available. A proselyting mission, followed by a leadership mission, followed by an educational mission, followed by a visitors' center mission, followed by a genealogy mission, followed by a welfare mission. If you ever get tired of serving the missions that keep you hopping, why not try a temple mission to a foreign land? Can't you sense that there is as much opportunity to try new things as you have time and interest to try?

Some couples like to time their home stays to coincide with spring and summer. Many couples do not like the harsh winters so often found along the Wasatch Front in Utah. Therefore, they plan to finish their mission in March or April and prepare to leave again by October or November. Then they have had ample time to reacquaint themselves with the children and grandchildren, renew old friendships, encourage some of their friends to join them, and then are off again.

In order to avoid potential conflict, make sure both of you are on the same wavelength. If the husband wants to go, go, go, and the wife wants a little break and some time with the family, mutual consideration must be given to avoid contention. There isn't a specified number of missions a couple should serve. For some, one is about all they can do. For others, five or six is very doable.

Too many couples sit at home worrying about going too often. Go on your first mission now and let the subsequent missions unfold as you complete your first mission. If you spend too much time worrying about the future, you may find that your health deteriorates to the point where even a first mission is questionable. Many couples have been talking all of their lives about the chance to serve when retirement finally comes. Then when it comes time to submit the papers, there is a certain fear that causes them to postpone submitting the papers until they're more sure of themselves. Diving into a cool pool is very much like a mission. If you try to put your toe in a little at a time, you may talk yourself out of a refreshing swim. If you just jump in, after the first few seconds your body adjusts to the water temperature and you have a great time.

Some couples decide they want to start with the foreign missions while they are still relatively young and healthy, and work their way closer to home as the years pass. One of our favorite couples served in South Africa, then England, then Australia, and then California. They were already planning their next mission before our exit interview. From them we got our desire to serve after our children are raised and on their own.

Sometimes senior couples worry that their aged parents need them more at home than they are needed in the field. Many of our couples found other family members, ward members, and friends who gladly tended to the needs of their parents while they served. Many of those with parents who were still alive said their parents urged them to go on a mission rather than wait around until they died.

Although finances were a concern, none of our senior couples worried about being able to survive their multiple missions. Some used rather creative ways of financing their missions, which is talked about in another chapter. They considered that it was just as expensive to live at home as it was to live in the mission field. However, the good they knew they were doing was an added bonus they received for serving. We have visited many wards in Utah. Often the high priests in the elders quorum have enough talent sitting idly by to satisfy the needs of several missions. Many of the senior sisters of these high priests confided that they would gladly serve if their husbands would accept the call.

We have heard some pretty lame excuses from some high priests for not serving. When all the dust is settled, they will still be one-year older next year. Wouldn't it be eternally worthwhile to have a year of service in the mission field to your list of credits rather than just another year of watching the grass grow? We wonder how many elders quorums would even know you were gone if you left unannounced tomorrow. How vital are you, really, to the running of the ward? Whatever your answer is, it pales in comparison to how valuable you will be in the mission field.

Why not conclude now to submit your papers for your first (and maybe your only!) mission? Then make your decision about future missions after you have a basis for your decision. Even senior couples can make rash statements about serving only one mission that they gladly retract later on.

NOTES

1. Russell M. Nelson, *Ensign*, May 1988, 35.
2. Gordon B. Hinckley, *Ensign*, November 1988, 52.

Chapter 19

WHAT TO DO WITH THINGS AT HOME

After a lifetime of accumulating, what are you going to do with all your stuff? That is no easy question to answer. Without sounding fatalistic at all, why not rephrase the question, "What would your family do with all that stuff if you were to pass away?" There are some exciting options available to you.

A mission motivates many senior couples into making moves they have talked about for years. Many couples are still living in the home where they raised their children. Since the children have all married and moved away, it seems like a lot of house for just the two of them. Have you talked about selling the house and moving to a smaller one or even into a condominium or a senior living center? Perhaps you are ready to let someone else do the yard work or the gardening. Many couples decide that now is a good time to purchase a spot in a retirement community. There is someone to watch your property and provide security even though you are not there.

You may be asking, "How do we know where we want to live when we return?" That is a legitimate question that may not be easily answered. It may not have to be answered until you return. Have you considered putting your household goods in storage while you serve and then wait until you return to see how you feel about where to live?

Putting things in storage has an additional advantage: it requires you to sort through your stuff before you decide what you want to keep and what you want to give away.

Boxing everything up also helps you organize for a future move. Some of those hidden treasures have been around for years. If you really needed them, chances are you would have to purchase them because, although you know you have them, you have no idea where they actually are. Going through those hidden treasures often gives you the opportunity to bless the lives of a newly married grandchild. What is certainly surplus storage for you may be a lifesaver for them.

Often a son or daughter will have sufficient space in their outbuilding or basement so that you won't have to pay the monthly fee for using secured storage areas. Ask the questions before you make a decision. You may be happily surprised to see the willingness of children to help you sort through, box up, throw out, and otherwise take care of your earthly belongings.

Many senior elders have been farmers all their lives. You have worked the ground, tended the flocks, mended the fences, repaired the barns, and taken care of essential chores all of your lives. You may have been so tied down with livestock that you have rarely taken a vacation because it has been too much of a hassle to get someone to care for the animals. Now might be a good time to sell your sheep and turn your attention to taking care of the "Master's sheep."

Although it often is a shock to the system, haven't you been talking about selling the farm and enjoying your golden years by doing something other than the endless tasks necessary to maintain a farm? Perhaps a child or grandchild would like to take over for you. You can carry the contract on the farm yourselves and generate enough cash to finance missions until you are at least one hundred and fifty years old!

Even if you are not ready to part with the farm, you may allow a son or grandson to take over for you while you are gone. In more than one incident, senior couples have concluded, after being away from the farm for a year or more, that they really don't want to go back to it. If you find that to be the case and you don't have anyone in the family who wants to go into farming, you can always have someone at home put the farm on the market for sale. You will be amazed at how much your land is worth. Unless you have had it appraised recently, you had better sit down before you open the appraisal letter.

If you don't have a family member who wants to run the farm, often a neighbor will keep things in shape by running it with his farm. Don't limit your opportunity to serve based on the idea that you are too tied to the land to serve. Where there is a will, the Lord will inspire you to find a way of serving without losing everything you have worked so hard to accumulate.

If you are in business, the same principles apply. Occasionally, senior couples just close the doors and don't worry about selling the business. Although it may cost you some money to do that, you may have also financially benefited greatly from your efforts over the years. Perhaps rather than go through the worry of selling and having someone ruin the reputation you have earned by your honesty, you may want to just close up shop. The choice is yours. There isn't a right or a wrong. Every couple is different.

We have witnessed what we thought were catastrophes. People purchased businesses and then while the couple served, the new owner ran the businesses into the ground. When the couple returned home, they didn't have much to show for their efforts. In each of the cases we are familiar with, the Lord has greatly prospered the returned senior couples. Within a short time they have been able to take over the business and had it back to its original level of productivity—often to a much higher degree of productivity than when they sold it.

Some of you may be involved as part owners in businesses. Often it is possible to become a silent partner for the time you are away. More often than not, the dividend checks keep coming in and the Lord prospers your business more because of your missionary service than while you were giving it your full attention. If leaving your position on the board of directors is not an option, then you are faced with the decision of resigning and letting someone else assume your responsibilities.

From our own personal experience, it is not wise to try to continue to run a business while doing your missionary work. The Lord requires that those who go "serve him with all their heart, might, mind, and strength, and with an eye single to his glory" (D&C 4:2–4). It is impossible to have your heart and head at home at the same time you are giving your undivided attention to missionary matters.

We have never talked to a senior missionary who was forced to sell a business who felt they had made the wrong choice. We have talked to several who admitted that it complicated their missions greatly because of their business ventures at home. You may decide to hire a professional manager for your business. He or she would be an expert who, for a salary, would watch out for your interests. You may discover when you return that they are actually doing a better job than you did and decide to keep them on full time. You may want to incentivize them by giving them a percentage of the business profits. The more they make for you, the more they make. Both of you are then winners.

In selling your home, farm, or business, make sure you contact a good tax consultant. If you purchased them long ago or at a greatly reduced price (as compared to today's prices), you could be stuck with a huge capital gains tax unless you handle your estate properly. Even though it may cost you a couple hundred dollars, it would be worth every penny to maximize your profits and minimize your taxes.

Selling often takes time. Don't wait until the month or two before you want to leave to start the selling process. Contact a real estate agent now and let them give you a feel for how long it may take to sell your holdings. Even if a buyer can be found immediately, it may take some time to arrange financing. It would be a shame to still be in the middle of trying to close on your sale when you report to the MTC.

If you have a large parcel of land, you may want to consider subdividing and selling the lots when it is most advantageous for you financially. All that farm land may one day be housing tracts. If you sell them all at once, the government will require you to pay a large portion of the profits as taxes. If you have a good tax consultant, he may be able to help you structure your income so that it isn't all eaten up in taxes. A good attorney or financial manager may save you thousands of dollars and a huge headache. Let them administer the sale of the lots, the collecting of the rents, and the payment of taxes, while you are free to serve.

Perhaps now would also be a good time to set up a family trust or at least have a will drawn up. Don't leave, until your dying breath, the details about what to do with your estate. As a land surveyor, I have seen too many families torn apart because the parents did not want to take the time to consider the distribution of their estate. One wonderful but not very sound-thinking grandmother said, "Oh, I'll just let the kids fight over it!" Since I was in the middle of trying to settle her estate, I knew that her statement was more prophetic than she ever imagined. The children would not even speak to one another and would only speak through me, even though we were all in the same room together. What should have been a time of enriching her children and grandchildren ended up impoverishing them as a family. Not so much financially as socially, emotionally, and spiritually. With that one thoughtless statement, she had literally destroyed the solidarity of her family. I often wondered if she was kicking herself from the spirit world because she didn't take action while she had the power to control the distribution of her goods.

Again, a good financial planner may be one of the most important people in your lives at that point. Sure, it will cost you a few hundred dollars to have him investigate all of the options available to you, but it could save you thousands of dollars at the time your estate is settled. Some families have added the names of their children on the deeds to their properties to help protect their possessions in the event of an unexpected death. The options are many, but without consulting someone with some training, most of those options may not be apparent to you.

Estate planning is one of the true joys of families who take charge of their lives. Probating an estate is one of the most frustrating events in the lives of descendants whose loved ones have not taken adequate forethought. What a bonding, uniting event to call the children together and take inventory of your worldly goods. You can ascertain at that time any wishes they may have and also dictate your desires in the presence of everyone. Such a simple meeting can avert relationship-destroying confrontations after your passing.

We do not want to give the impression that your passing is imminent, just that a mission provides a golden opportunity for you to do something that you really need to give attention to, and something that will greatly solidify your family.

Chapter 20

SERVING IN THE TEMPLE OR SERVING A MISSION?

The Church has a single mission—to bring souls unto Christ. Within that mission statement are four phases: perfecting the Saints, redeeming the dead, proclaiming the gospel, and caring for the poor and needy. One is not more important than another. All of them will require our greatest effort to successfully prepare the world for the millennial day. There is ample need for workers in all four areas. Perhaps, then, it isn't so much a decision of which area to focus on as much as which one to focus on at this particular time. The Prophet Joseph Smith prioritized our responsibilities when he said, "After all that has been said, the greatest and most important duty is to preach the Gospel."[1]

As the gospel continued to be revealed "line upon line, precept upon precept" (D&C 98:12), the Prophet further revealed: "The greatest responsibility in this world that God has laid upon us is to seek after our dead. The Apostle Paul says, 'They without us cannot be made perfect;' (Hebrews 11:40) for it is necessary that the sealing power should be in our hands to seal our children and our dead for the fulness of the dispensation of times — a dispensation to meet the promises made by Jesus Christ before the foundation of the world for the salvation of man."[2]

It is apparent that one aspect of the mission of the Church does not take precedence over the other three. However, it is possible to do both temple work and missionary work while we continue working on perfecting the Saints and watching out for the poor and needy. It would be a tragedy of the first order if every senior couple in the Church quit their jobs in the temples to leave on missions. Fortunately that is hardly a worry we must contend with. But there are thousands of able-bodied senior couples who could take a leave from their Christ-like temple work to give some attention to the charge to proclaim the gospel.

From a very pragmatic point of view, the state of physical wellness required of a person to work in the temple is less than the requirement for missionary service. If the ability to stand, walk, climb stairs, and work for sustained periods of time is already compromised, then temple work is likely the most viable option. However, before that state of physical deterioration is reached, many senior couples could easily serve one or more missions.

Consider one rather obvious fact: the dead aren't going anywhere until the ordinances are performed in their behalf. The living, however, are one day closer to death today than they were yesterday. Therefore, we have one less day today to teach them and allow them to perform the saving and exalting ordinances for themselves than we had yesterday. The fact that the ordinances are essential for exaltation is not the question. Every son or daughter of Adam and Eve who arrives at the age of accountability and knows the difference between right and wrong must have those ordinances performed before they can enter into the presence of the Lord in the celestial kingdom.

Continue to investigate the advantage of doing missionary work while you have the strength and stamina to do it. If you diligently go to the temple and perform every ordinance humanly possible, you are limited by the number of hours in a day. If you were successful in going on a mission and converting twenty people, and they all followed through and received their own endowments and then became temple workers, you have increased by twenty times the number of vicarious ordinances you are directly responsible for performing. If, in turn, those twenty people happened to be ten senior couples (which is not unlikely since senior people are more likely to listen to people their own age than to the younger missionaries) and if each of those ten couples went on missions and converted twenty more people, you can see how the amount of temple work you are directly credited for having performed increases exponentially.

There is no question that the work for the dead is crucial and must be done before they can be liberated from the prison-like environment they are confined to in the spirit world. But the limiting factor in how much work can be done is the number of mortals who are willing to serve in the temples and do vicarious work for the dead. There are virtually millions of senior couples out there who are not yet members of the Church who could spend countless hours in the holy temples doing temple work for the dead *if* they were members of the Church. Many of them are already prepared to join the Church but for one problem—there is no one to teach them.

The Lord declared that there are many who were now ready to receive the gospel: "For there are many yet on the earth among all sects, parties, and denominations, who are blinded by the subtle craftiness of men, whereby they lie in wait to deceive, and who are only kept from the truth because they know not where to find it" (D&C 123:12).

While it is true that there are tens of thousands of missionaries currently serving missions for the Church, that is only a fraction of the number needed. At that rate, every missionary would have to contact and teach more than 95,000 people in order to teach everyone on the earth. That is physically impossible. As great as the young people are, there are many people, who because of their false pride, will not listen to them because of their youth. There is something about gray hair or no hair that adds status to a person.

There is a time and a season to everything under the sun (see Ecclesiastes 3:1–8). There was a time when you were younger that you could run and jump, climb trees, and scale mountains. There was a time when you were to court and marry. There was a time when you were to bear and rear children. There was a time when the children were to leave the home and strike out on their own. There came a time when some of the things you did before (or were supposed to do) were no longer possible for you. There was a time when you were to work full-time to earn a living and provide the necessities of life. Then there came a time when providing for the basics was not the all-consuming task that it had been for years. Now is the time for us to put our lives in order and share what we have learned and experienced over a lifetime with those who were not so privileged as we are. There will yet come a time when we will not be able to serve missions with the same vigor we can now. Then will be the time when we should consider wearing out our lives in temple service and serving local missions or less physically demanding missions.

For many, this idea of maximizing our investment is no more than broadening a concept we have dealt with for years. In investing our money, it was always desirable to get the greatest return for the lowest amount of risk. Now as we consider carefully the remaining years of our lives, we would do well to perform a like asset analysis. Where would be the greatest return on our time and energy? Although the thoughts of going on a mission may be frightening to some, it also promises the greatest return with the lowest risk.

Many of us are descendants of pioneers who left all to follow the invitation of a prophet to migrate to the West. Many of us are beneficiaries of those who sacrificed all to join the Church and gather with the Saints to establish Zion. What would have been the results for you and your family if some missionary had been unwilling to leave their comfort zone and go on a mission? The answer is obvious—we wouldn't be members of the Church.

Now consider one other very sobering fact: If the gospel were removed from your life entirely, what difference would it make to you and your family? The thought is staggering to us. Our entire lives are influenced by the gospel. It is difficult to envision life without the gospel. But millions are experiencing what is like a nightmare thought to us—life without the gospel influence.

The dead are not in a position to experience continued life on earth without the gospel. They have already passed through this stage of their immortal trek and moved on to the next apartment. There they will be taught and, hopefully, accept the fulness of the gospel. But their accepting the gospel there will not influence their lives in mortality, because they won't be coming back for a re-run on life. Therefore, the impact of the gospel (which is tremendous) will be experienced in an immortal state.

Our plea is to take full advantage of your time now to help those who are still in a position to enjoy the mortal as well as the immortal benefits of the gospel. Join the army of the Lord in doing work to secure the salvation of the living, and then let's turn our attention to the salvation of the dead.

Whatever part of the four aspects of Church service you engage in, you will be greatly blessed. The Lord said: "Wherefore, go ye and preach my gospel, whether to the north or to the south, to the east or to the west, it mattereth not, for ye cannot go amiss" (D&C 80:3). Preaching the gospel could narrowly be interpreted as proclaiming the gospel. More broadly, however, it would include helping to perfect the Saints who are already members of the Church. It could also include the follow-up work to the missionary work that is currently being done in the spirit world—redeeming the dead. Many of those you will be working with will fall into the fourth category, poor and needy. They seem to be the ones who are most apt to listen to the gospel.

Whichever area of the kingdom you are currently involved in, it will be a blessing to you and your family. One cannot listen to Sunday School teachers teach the youth or adults without knowing that the labors they are performing, although often very frustrating, are essential to the continued growth of the Church. One cannot attend the temple and feel the sweet prevailing spirit that is there without knowing for sure that temple work is ordained of God. Great appreciation comes via the Spirit to those who sacrifice their lives in performing ordinances for and in behalf of the dead. Anyone who has ever been involved in missionary work can readily testify that there are no greater rewards than those experienced by missionaries who give their all to spread the gospel to the children of our Heavenly Father who, at present, are not privileged to enjoy all the benefits we now enjoy.

How great will be our joy with one soul we have aided in gaining eternal life whether as a missionary, a teacher, or a temple worker.

There is not, and indeed should not be, competition between these four vital parts of the Church's mission. But there are choices that must be made if you are going to enjoy the blessings of serving a full-time mission. Consider carefully your options and let the Holy Spirit guide your choice.

NOTES

1. *Teachings of the Prophet Joseph Smith,* 112.
2. Ibid., 356.

Chapter 21

SETTING AN EXAMPLE FOR OUR FAMILIES

John, the ancient and beloved apostle, once said, "I have no greater joy than to hear that my children walk in truth" (3 John 1:4). What parent, who really understands the great plan of salvation, wouldn't sacrifice all that they have to ensure that their children and grandchildren are secure in the gospel? There are many things you could do to secure your children and grandchildren to you. There is almost an automatic bond between grandparents and their grandchildren. Something about Grandma's cooking or Grandpa's stories doesn't seem to require anything else to endear grandchildren to you.

However, the love we have for them may be based on the love they freely give to us. Is there something you might do for them that would be more powerful in cementing that love? There is, and it is simply this: Let them sacrifice for you! If you haven't noticed, this generation is not notorious for being self-sacrificing. Many are very self-centered. They have serious "I" problems. They almost always ask for or at least look for the answer to "what's in it for me?"

When you decide to go on a mission, something bordering on miraculous happens. Yes, they are going to have to give up the Sunday dinners, the treats, the visits to, the holidays with, and the constant presence of their grandparents. But in addition to that they are going to start being more worried about your safety and well-being than they have ever been before. Prayers that may have been rather routine will suddenly take on an air of seriousness and sincerity never before seen. Elder Vaughan J. Featherstone identified this same principle: "Thousands of mature couples and widowed missionaries could be called if they would simply make themselves available. Many of us understand the blessings that come when children and grandchildren kneel down at night and say, 'Dear Heavenly Father, please bless grandma and grandpa who are out in Texas on a mission.'"[1]

I want to bear a personal testimony of this principle. My father died when I was only four and a half years old. I had a very close relationship with my paternal grandparents. Grandpa Bott became almost like a substitute father to my older brother and me. When I was about ten years old, Grandpa and Grandma were called on a mission and assigned to work on a Navajo reservation in Arizona. I had grown up watching cowboy and Indian movies and was scared to death that my grandparents would be shot and scalped. Never in my young life had I prayed as often and as fervently for divine protection for the missionaries as I did for the two years that Grandpa and Grandma served. It virtually welded my soul to theirs.

They became my role models. From that time on, I knew that I wanted to serve a mission like Grandpa and Grandma. I read their letters with intense interest. I talked with them when they returned. I listened to them speak about their experiences. I looked endlessly at photo albums of them with their investigators and converts. I asked thousands of questions. Without realizing what they were doing, they focused my boyish attention on the blessings of serving a mission. I never recovered. I served a mission to Somoa as a young adult and later served missions to Hawaii and Sydney, Australia, with my sweetheart. I also served twice as a stake mission president and spent three years as a mission president in California. My wife and I are currently planning our next mission.

Would I say my grandparents' mission was worth it? Judge for yourself. Am I taking every effort to help others recognize the value of missionary service? Again, you must judge for yourself. I taught well over one thousand pre-missionaries every semester at BYU in the Sharing the Gospel classes. Both Grandpa and Grandma have since passed away, but the influence they had on me continues to linger. I will always be grateful that they set the example for me to follow.

How could a struggling grandson possibly say, "A mission is too much of a sacrifice!" when Grandpa and Grandma are serving? He is young and robust, and you may be hobbling along, barely able to negotiate stairs. The youth have sort of this super-ego thing about thinking everyone over thirty is nearing the grave. The older we get, the more inclined we are to smile at their self-centeredness. So, anything you can do, they can do better, faster, and with less effort. In one short mission you can erase forever their weak excuses for not serving.

Your weekly letters and emails to the family may be the determining factor to keep a grandson or granddaughter from making a moral mistake that would jeopardize their privilege of serving a mission or give them the strength to say "no" to drugs or alcohol.

Each semester I required my students in the Sharing the Gospel classes to write a paper about a spiritual experience that contributed to their conversion. Many papers dealt with the influence of grandparents at critical junctions during their lives. Several had noted how a letter or call from a grandparent at the point when they were seriously considering suicide had virtually saved their lives. I usually wrote on the bottom of their paper asking them if they had ever shared that experience with their grandparents. They would usually seek me out after the papers were returned and say they had never even thought to thank Grandpa or Grandma for their encouragement.

In the mission field you will be closer to the Lord than you have ever been. You will find that you are much more prone to listen to the whisperings of the Spirit. One of our senior elders was serving as a patriarch at the time of his mission call. He told me he didn't remember ever getting clearer direction from the Lord than during his mission.

With that increased sensitivity, you may be in the best position in the world to be a genuine help to your children and grandchildren.

Because life in the mission field is lived in the fast lane (as will be expounded upon in the next chapter), you will have so many more experiences to draw principles from in helping your family cope with the stresses of modern living. In almost every conceivable situation they may find themselves in, you have just encountered or know about one very similar. Drawing upon the experience you will gain in helping solve those problems, you will soon discover that you become a walking encyclopedia of gospel-based solutions to life's problems. What a blessing to have the wisdom of age and the experiences of a lifetime to bless your children during their times of struggle.

Often the reverses of life are difficult to understand when we are young and inexperienced. The older we get, the more our vision helps us keep the problems of life in proper perspective. For example, it is difficult to convince teenagers that "one little cigarette" will hurt them at all. For those of us who have witnessed the senseless destruction of human life, family life, or Church life associated with smoking, it isn't difficult to bear testimony that the Word of Wisdom revealed the potential problems associated with tobacco use long before modern science began its investigation.

In the world in which young people are growing up, immorality is portrayed in every movie, in every video, on the internet, in almost every magazine, and in almost every book they read. Hollywood tries to masquerade immorality as desirable, innocent, something everybody does, and a natural biological function having no eternal consequences. Never do they present the broken lives, the destroyed families, the loss of faith, the fear of what will happen now because the individual has offended God. It requires someone who has lived long enough to have watched the drama unfold to see how devastating immorality is to everything it touches. Being empowered by the Spirit, you, even more than their parents, will be able to warn your grandchildren about the potentially lethal effects of drugs, alcohol, tobacco, and unlicensed sex.

You represent two respected climbers who have successfully scaled the very mountain your family hopes to climb. They look to you in a way similar to the way they look to God—the difference being that you are visible to them, and they must learn to trust God by exercising faith. Since they envision you as standing on top of the mountain, they are more than willing to seek your advice on how to successfully climb it themselves. Don't underestimate the impact your counsel will have on their young lives.

They know, maybe even better than you are willing to admit, that your vision of the way things are and the way they ought to be, far exceeds their limited vision. This is a difficult time in the lives of parents. Perhaps you remember from your own experience, when children will listen to others before taking their parents' advice. One of the divinely instituted sources of sound, gospel-centered advice comes from grandparents. Being in the mission field seems to double the power of your counsel.

By sharing with them the challenges you are facing and the way you are facing those challenges, their confidence in the do-ability of their challenges increase. Not everybody is failing. Many of the young people of this generation seem to turn to drugs, alcohol, and sex because there seems to them no purpose or direction in their lives. Many sense that there is no future for them. When we listen to the news reports of all the gloom and doom, we are tempted to succumb to those same feelings. However, the gospel makes sense out of the struggles of life. We are fired with the vision of the future and do not despair because of the darkness of the storm clouds that surround us. Without sharing that vision with your family, many of them will weary of the length and difficulty of the battle and give up.

Notice the power you are given when you serve your mission and return home to encourage the grandchildren to serve. If you have chosen to stay at home, then when you encourage them to make the sacrifices necessary to serve a mission, they can easily come back and ask, "Why didn't you serve missions?" Even if you list a hundred good reasons, and even if you succeed in convincing them that it was just impossible for you to serve, they still have a powerful role model who did not serve.

Note the difference when you encourage them to serve and they ask (if they were too small to remember), "Did you serve?" The power comes when you lovingly take them in your arms and say, "Why, yes, sweetheart, your grandfather and I did serve a mission and it was the greatest experience of our entire lives!" What is to be said after that? You have made your point. In their language you've "been there, done that."

As we take a broader view of life, we sometimes fail to realize why we have so much confidence in the Savior as a guide. Paul taught a powerful truth concerning this matter: "For we have not an high priest which cannot be touched with the feeling of our infirmities; but was in all points tempted like as we are, yet without sin. Let us therefore come boldly unto the throne of grace, that we may obtain mercy, and find grace to help in time of need" (Hebrews 4:15–16).

No matter what our problems, no matter how difficult and challenging our temptations, we can go to the Savior in humble prayer and know that He will understand and have a sympathetic ear, because He's "been there, done that." The more like our Savior we become, the more confidence our children and grandchildren will have as they seek for help in overcoming their challenges.

Our willingness to act as role models for our family cannot be overemphasized. Your entire life is like a journey. By being willing to serve to the very end, you are closely following in the footsteps of the Master. Many of today's youth see life as an event with a great burst of speed and energy for a short period of time and then rest and relaxation until the end. They have as their role models rock stars who make millions of dollars on a single record or song. To them that is the ideal. Your Christ-paralleled life of total service and dedication is the most powerful influence we know to countermand the worldly model.

It seems like such a small sacrifice to insure such desirable results. There is really only one way to lead—by example. Why not fill out your mission papers today and continue your lifetime of setting the proper example?

NOTE

1. Vaughn J. Featherstone, *Ensign*, November 1978, 26.

Chapter 22

A LIFETIME OF MEMORIES

While serving as mission president, we had two daughters serve missions. Each week we would write letters to let them know what had been going on. Often it would require twice as many stamps as a normal letter required because of the volume of things we had to write about. We thought it was because we were mission president and had so many activities and missionaries to take care of. Then one day we mentioned our plight to the senior couples. To our surprise they said exactly the same thing! Their lives were so full that it seemed impossible to keep a journal and write weekly letters.

The answer to the dilemma may be in a statement made by our Area Presidency. They reported that the General Authorities calculated that a well-served two year mission was equivalent to fifty years of normal Church service! That would calculate to an astounding thirty-seven and a half years of experiences in just a year and a half! It is no wonder that it seems like life is lived in the fast lane in the mission field.

It would seem that because each day only has a limit of twenty-four hours, no matter whether you were at home or in the mission field, the same number of events would transpire. Although it is readily admitted that everyone's day had only twenty-four hours, that is where the logic breaks down. At home there was probably a routine. Get up, have breakfast, go to work, break for lunch, work the rest of the day, come home for supper, relax for the evening, then go to bed. Not too much to really get excited about other than an occasional difference in sequence.

In the mission field the only constant is knowing that every day will be different. One day you may help branch leaders work on records. The next day you may help a new mother tend her children while her husband goes for groceries. More likely you'll both tend children and go for the groceries. A third day you may spend most of the day trying to find lost members. They are not lost to themselves; the Church just doesn't know where they are! Instead of that being a regular day, each visit brings a new adventure that requires reporting. You'll have inspiration that will astound you on what to say to these total strangers to immediately cause them to love and trust you. You will spend half the night explaining to your journal the mind-expanding insights you received during a discussion to a second less active. You may likely feel frustrated because you want to record promptings you had at a third home that brought a flood of tears when the people said you had told them the exact thing they had dreamed the night before.

Another day it may be working with the local people on the stake welfare farm, visiting the sick in the hospital, helping someone fill out job applications, intercede in a potentially explosive confrontation among branch members, attend a spiritually uplifting zone conference with the mission president, make arrangements for a baptismal service, help a new member fill out a family group sheet, take a sick member to see the doctor, talk to a minister from another church who had spread false rumors about what you were doing, follow up on a dozen referrals you received from the mission office, bake a cake for a Relief Society meeting, and the list goes endlessly on.

Just about the time you think you have exhausted the diversity of what missionary life is all about, you get a call to give a blessing to a sick child of a less active member, the young missionaries need you to accompany them while they teach a single sister, the branch president asks you to take the entire sacrament meeting speaking time because he forgot to ask anyone to speak, the Primary chorister isn't sure how to lead 6/8 time, you get a call at 3:00 a.m. from a panicked investigator whose son has just been jailed for distribution of a controlled substance and they need your help, you get a call from the mission president who wants you to help solve a companion dispute between two young missionaries, you have reports due to the district leader, you are asked to organize a youth chorus for district conference, you are assigned a twenty-minute talk for zone development meeting, you teach the final new member discussions to a family who was recently baptized, or you are preparing a family for their first trip to the temple. Before long the mind begins to reel and you begin to wonder whether you can keep up.

Then you realize that you've only just begun! You are reading scriptures together and receive some insight on how to help a wayward child or grandchild at home. You need to write a quick letter before the thought escapes you. Right then you get the impression to visit a member on the far side of your area. You realize that the Spirit is prompting you so you leave immediately, only to arrive there in time to rescue the sleeping family from their flaming house. On the way home you stop at the family history center to help a new member find a lost ancestor. You arrive home only to discover that you don't have any food in the refrigerator. At the grocery store the stocker asks why you are wearing badges. You briefly explain and then set up a follow-up visit to give his family the first discussion. You arrive home and listen to your voice mail. The other couples want you to meet for family home evening and then go out for ice cream. You are about ready for some much needed rest and the phone rings. It is a family who had started taking the lessons a few months ago but had lost interest. They have just had an experience that frightened them and wonder if you could come over and talk to them. The young missionaries want to hold a special birthday dinner at your place—they will provide the food if you'll cook the meal. Your most golden investigator received some anti-Mormon literature and is really wavering and wants to know if you can meet with her and answer some questions. You get a telephone call wanting to change your appointment to a time when you already have an appointment scheduled so you tell them you'll call back and see if you can rearrange the second appointment. You discover that you haven't had time to do the laundry for the past two weeks so you have no clean clothes. An unwed girl in your branch needs someone to go with her to the hospital to deliver her baby. The adoption agency calls immediately after asking you to provide post-adoption counseling to the young mother. Just when you are sure you are going to die of sensory overload, you get a phone call informing you that a young father has just been killed in an automobile accident, leaving a wife and four little children. Could you pay them a visit and explain life after death?

If you think we are exaggerating, you are in for a shock. This really is just the tip of the iceberg. During the three years that we served, the only day we could even semi-count on to be normal was transfer day. That was predictable because we knew something would always go wrong!

By the time you get a week into your mission you will realize that in order to get thirty-seven and a half years of experience crammed into a year and a half, events are going to have to happen in multiple doses, at the same time, and with little or no time in between. Don't despair. The Lord will strengthen you so you can handle all this and much more. Several of our couples would discuss which part of the day each was to write about so they could capture the majority of the events of the day without duplicating their efforts.

Then how do you find time to fit it all in? We don't know, you just do. The Lord really does increase your organizational abilities. Even couples who worried out loud during the entrance interview about their inability to remember often commented how much clearer their minds worked and how much better their memories were.

You may believe that we are exaggerating our point, but listen to what our leaders are saying. First Elder David B. Haight quotes senior couples he interviewed about some of their experiences:

> After teaching a young couple to read, or seeing the happiness in a family because the father was again attending Church, we would walk back to our little apartment with a heart that was singing and feet that hardly touched the cobblestone street. Seeing a young mother clap her hands with joy as she truly realized that she was reading, or watching a

> baby and knowing that perhaps this child wouldn't be alive now had we not been serving in that city at that time. These experiences, each and every one, made our mission worth every minute of it.[1]

Elder L. Tom Perry in April 1984 general conference said:

> I have especially been impressed with the older couples who, after fulfilling a life of service in their wards and stakes, have the desire to spend a period of time as missionaries in full service to the Lord. I have found them in all corners of the world, and they are, I guess, the happiest people I have ever met because of what they are accomplishing. Let me just share parts of some letters written by those who have had this great privilege. These quotations are from a composite of letters. They were written to their mission president and his wife after the couples had been serving in the mission field for some time.[2]

Then Elder Perry reports some of the experiences senior couples shared with him. The purpose of including this quote is to show you that these senior couples were among the "happiest people I've ever met." The richness of your experience is not dependent on whether you serve in a foreign land among native people with strange customs and exotic foods, on a Native American reservation in Arizona, or among the Southeast Asians in California. Wherever you go, you are in for the time of your lives.

All of these experiences will be eclipsed by the love you will develop for the people you serve. When you return home, it will be necessary to either get a job or curb the number of phone calls you make back to your beloved friends. You will find that although your mission will come to an end, the memories will not. Not infrequently you will enjoy visits from your mission friends. You will find the conversations you have over the breakfast table will be about experiences you shared as a couple in the mission field. You will receive gifts at Christmas time and for your birthday. You will display a wall of memorabilia you brought from the mission field. You may even have decided, as did one of our choice couples, to write a book about your experience. And believe us—you'll have plenty to write about.

We have talked with couples who returned from their missions ten years ago. They still talk as though their mission was yesterday. When asked, they readily admitted that not a day goes by that they don't think and talk about their mission. Some even report that their children ask if they can talk about something other than their mission! However, since that will likely be the richest experiences of your lives, you will want to talk about it with everyone you meet. You'll be asked to give firesides and to talk at club meetings. You may be asked to speak in stake conferences and sacrament meetings. Relief Society lessons and priesthood lessons dealing with seniors serving missions will be turned directly over to you. You will find yourselves talking freely to your grandchildren and the neighborhood children about the value of serving a mission. Without hesitation, we can promise that your entire life's focus will change as a result of your mission.

It will not be unusual that your most staunch supporters upon the passing of your companion will be missionaries who served with you—both the senior variety and the younger missionaries. Mission reunions will be a treasured experience as long as you care to attend. You will never tire of reliving those truly golden years you spent in the mission field.

Is your treasure chest of cherished memories too full to add another life time's worth of memories? Why not double your memories by serving a mission? Even those difficult times will become treasured experiences long to be cherished. The Lord is waiting to bless you with everything we have mentioned and more. Put Him to the test.

NOTES

1. David B. Haight, *Ensign*, May 1987, 61.
2. L. Tom Perry, *Ensign*, May 1984, 79.

Chapter 23

THE PROMISED REWARDS OF MISSIONARY SERVICE

Do we have to anticipate a reward for serving a mission? No. That isn't the reason we serve. We serve because we love the Lord and want to demonstrate that love by our obedience to His commandments. However, promises are made to those who serve Him and will come as a side benefit from selfless service. In this chapter we will discuss only a few. As you study the scriptures, especially the Doctrine and Covenants, you will be amazed at the promises the Lord makes for serving in the mission field.

Ancient King Benjamin, in his final address to his beloved people, taught a truth that applies to your service as missionaries:

> I say unto you that if ye should serve him who has created you from the beginning, and is preserving you from day to day, by lending you breath, that ye may live and move and do according to your own will, and even supporting you from one moment to another—I say, if ye should serve him with all your whole souls yet ye would be unprofitable servants. And behold, all that he requires of you is to keep his commandments; and he has promised you that if ye would keep his commandments ye should prosper in the land; and he never doth vary from that which he hath said; therefore, if ye do keep his commandments he doth bless you and prosper you. And now, in the first place, he hath created you, and granted unto you your lives, for which ye are indebted unto him. And secondly, he doth require that ye should do as he hath commanded you; for which if ye do, **he doth immediately bless you**;

> and therefore he hath paid you. And ye are still indebted unto him, and are, and will be, forever and ever; therefore, of what have ye to boast? (Mosiah 2:21–24, emphasis added).

The point we want to emphasize is that He "doth immediately bless you." Sometimes we view the blessings for our labors as something we will receive in the world to come. While it is true that many blessings will be fully realized in the life to come, there are many that are earmarked specifically for this life.

When the rich young man asked the Savior what he needed to do to gain eternal life, the Savior admonished him to keep the commandments. Upon his declaration that he already was compliant with the commandments the Savior had outlined for him, the Savior then invited him, as a final prerequisite to gaining eternal life, to "go thy way, sell whatsoever thou hast, and give to the poor, and thou shalt have treasure in heaven: and come, take up the cross, and follow me" (Mark 10:21). As you recall, the young man went away sorrowing because his heart was so fixed on the things of this world that he was unwilling to make the sacrifice.

Peter asked the question we all want to know the answer to: What's in it for us who have forsaken everything and followed thee? The Savior gave a promise which only He can fulfill: "And Jesus answered and said, Verily I say unto you, There is no man that hath left house, or brethren, or sisters, or father, or mother, or wife, or children, or lands, for my sake, and the gospel's, but he shall receive an hundredfold now in this time, houses, and brethren, and sisters, and mothers, and children, and lands, with persecutions; and in the world to come eternal life" (Mark 10:29–30).

The Lord said the faithful missionary servant would receive an hundred fold of houses and lands—physical blessings. One hundred-fold of brethren, sisters, wives, and children. Some may be thinking: "I don't want to have a hundred wives or a hundred children!" Perhaps He is promising that because of our missionary service our relationship with our husbands, wives, children, and grandchildren will be a hundred times better than it would have been had we chosen not to serve. Additionally, the acquaintances you will make in the mission field will become like family members—sometimes you discover that you are closer to them than you are to members of your own family!

I don't know of any stock on the stock market, any business in the financial world, or any legitimate venture where you can receive a hundred times your investment in just a year or a year and a half. Ponder the scripture and see if you can find an alternate meaning. We have, and the meaning seems to be authoritatively stated and not subject to multiple interpretations.

Finally, the Savior promises eternal life in the world to come. Since that is our ultimate goal, what greater activity can we participate in that will guarantee a seat in the celestial kingdom than missionary work?

Without entering a doctrinal discourse on making one's calling and election sure, may we reiterate a promise made to Thomas B. Marsh. He had been plagued by problems within his family. The Lord recognized Thomas' suffering and promised that one day his family would see the light and join with him in the Church (see D&C 31:2). Later in that same revelation, the Lord promised: "Therefore, thrust in your sickle with all your soul, and your sins are forgiven you, and you shall be laden with sheaves upon your back, for the laborer is worthy of his hire. Wherefore, **your family shall live**. Behold, verily I say unto you, go from them only for a little time, and declare my word, and I will prepare a place for them" (D&C 31:5–6, emphasis added).

Two promises leap out at the senior missionaries: (1) your family shall live and (2) the Lord will take care of our families. The Prophet Joseph Smith enlarged upon this concept. He said: "Four destroying angels holding power over the four quarters of the earth until the servants of God are sealed in their foreheads, which signifies sealing the blessing upon their heads, meaning the everlasting covenant, thereby making their calling and election made sure. When a seal is put upon the father and mother, it secures their posterity, so that they cannot be lost, but will be saved by virtue of the covenant of their father and mother."[1]

When one ponders Peter's step-by-step process for making one's calling and election sure as found in 2 Peter 1, one cannot help but note the similarity between that list and the list revealed to the Prophet Joseph Smith in Doctrine and Covenants 4:5–6. Those listed in the Doctrine and Covenants are the prerequisites for being successful as missionaries. Could it possibly be that daily laboring in the Lord's vineyard is the fastest way of making one's calling and election sure? And by so doing, do we not qualify to have our children sealed to us so they cannot be lost, as the Prophet promised?

As you contemplate the above scriptures and quotes, can you avoid seeing that serving a mission may well be the most eternally significant thing you can possibly do as a couple? One gets the idea that the Savior is very serious about His desire to bless those who serve Him.

The blessings of promised protection for you while in His service are many. Perhaps a single reference will be representative of the blessings you will receive as you serve. "And whoso receiveth you, there I will be also, for I will go before your face. I will be on your right hand and on your left, and my Spirit shall be in your hearts, and mine angels round about you, to bear you up" (D&C 84:88).

Consider for a moment the magnitude of this promise. The pronoun "I" here is the Savior Himself. He has promised to go before you and be on your right hand and on your left. The wonderful Revelator (the Holy Ghost) is promised to be in your heart. And if that is not sufficient, the Savior even promises that angels will be round about you to bear you up. That sounds like pretty good company to us!

You will discover as you study the scriptures together, and particularly as you teach your beloved investigators, that you feel a presence stronger than you ever have before. You can expect it. "Verily, verily, I say unto you, as I said unto my disciples, where two or three are gathered together in my name, as touching one thing, behold, there will I be in the midst of them—even so am I in the midst of you" (D&C 6:32). From our own and the experience of countless missionaries, including senior couples, we testify of the veracity of this promise.

In various chapters in this book we have mentioned blessings that will happen to you as you teach. Remember Doctrine and Covenants 71:9—no weapon formed against you shall prosper. Remember Doctrine and Covenants 84:85 and 100:5–8—that it shall be given to you in the very hour, even in the very moment, what you shall say. In conjunction with these verses the Lord promised earlier: "Yea, open your mouths and spare not, and you shall be laden with sheaves upon your backs, for lo, I am with you" (D&C 33:9). In verses 8 and 10 of the same section, the command is given to "open your mouths" with specific promises associated with each command.

The Lord makes this classic connection with the bearing of one's testimony. "Nevertheless, ye are blessed, for the testimony which ye have borne is recorded in heaven for the angels to look upon; and they rejoice over you, and your sins are forgiven you" (D&C 62:3). I have never met a humble, sincere person who didn't long to know that his or her sins had been forgiven. Here is a sure-fire method.

As we have mentioned throughout the book, missions are not easy. Perhaps it will be the most difficult thing you have ever done as a couple. But it will also be the most rewarding. Note again the association the Lord makes with sacrificing and forgiveness of sins: "Behold, I have seen your sacrifices, and will forgive all your sins; I have seen your sacrifices in obedience to that which I have told you. Go, therefore, and I make a way for your escape, as I accepted the offering of Abraham of his son Isaac" (D&C 132:50). Not only are we promised a forgiveness of sins but also a way to escape the hands of our persecutors, persecutions, and unseen pitfalls of life. Can we really consider not going?

Hyrum Smith, the Prophet's older brother, wanted so badly to share what he was learning with the people around him who were perishing for want of gospel knowledge. The Lord gave a wonderful missionary revelation to him which is relevant to our discussion from the first verse to the last. You may desire to read Doctrine and Covenants 11 as a couple. Part of what the Lord said was, "Verily, verily, I say unto you, even as you desire of me so it shall be done unto you; and, if you desire, you shall be the means of doing much good in this generation. Say nothing but repentance unto this generation. Keep my commandments, and assist to bring forth my work, according to my commandments, and you shall be blessed" (D&C 11:8–9).

What are the desires of your hearts? Even as we desire of Him, so shall it be unto us. It is as though He is literally saying, "You want it, you've got it!" It would be a terrible tragedy to stand with the Savior on the other side of the veil in review of our mortal existence only to discover that we had set our sights too low.

We don't know of any other time during life when so much focus is put on keeping the commandments of the Lord. Even some of the little things that are not necessarily against the commandments, but we know we will have to overcome them before entering the celestial kingdom, come into clear focus. The increased presence of the Spirit has a profound effect on you as a missionary.

> And now, verily, verily, I say unto thee, put your trust in that Spirit which leadeth to do good—yea, to do justly, to walk humbly, to judge righteously; and this is my Spirit. Verily, verily, I say unto you, I will impart unto you of my Spirit, which shall enlighten your mind, which shall fill your soul with joy; And then shall ye know, or by this shall you know, all things whatsoever you desire of me, which are pertaining unto things of righteousness, in faith believing in me that you shall receive. (D&C 11:12–14)

Note the promised blessings: you'll have a greater desire to do good and be good. To deal justly with each other and your fellow men. To walk humbly rather than being proud, self-centered, and difficult to live with. The Spirit also enlightens your mind and gives you insights that, without the help of the Spirit, you cannot gain. The Spirit will fill your soul with joy, not sorrow and sadness at being separated from your familiar surroundings and family. In addition to all those very positive and desirable blessings, the Lord said that by the power of the Spirit we could know anything we wanted to know concerning things of righteousness—how to perfect ourselves, our families, our wards and branches, and our friends. Most of us are fairly adept at identifying *what* needs to be improved. It is infinitely more difficult to know *how* to improve things.

It is difficult to read those early sections of the Doctrine and Covenants without being amazed at the promises the Lord has made to those who thrust in their sickle with their might. "Behold, the field is white already to harvest; therefore, whoso desireth to reap, let him thrust in his sickle with his might, and reap while the day lasts, that he may treasure up for his soul everlasting salvation in the kingdom of God" (D&C 6:3).

The fastest, most efficient way of ensuring everlasting salvation for yourselves and your loved ones is to go on a mission. Again, we challenge you: Put the Lord to the test and see if He does not fulfill all of His promises to you both in this life and in the life to come.

NOTE

1. *Teachings of the Prophet Joseph Smith*, 321.

Chapter 24

SUNBIRDS OR SAVING ANGELS?

This chapter is not intended to lay a guilt trip on anyone or make light of those who choose to move South to avoid the cold winters where they live. It is our hope that a comparison of contrasting lifestyles will facilitate the decision-making process as you decide to serve a mission.

Occasionally we had the opportunity to travel to the southern part of the United States for Know Your Religion lectures. We always enjoyed the warm reception we received not only by the people who attend the lectures but also by the mild temperatures. After enduring a long winter of snow and cold, it was almost impossible to describe what it felt like to walk around in short sleeves and pick oranges and lemons from the trees. Although only an hour or slightly more away from home by airplane, we felt like it was a different world.

On a trip to Arizona, we had occasion to interface with an unusually large number of retired couples who were enjoying the winter in a retirement community. After attending the lecture, they excitedly told us about their accommodations and the arrangements they had with the community organization to watch out for their trailer houses while they were away during the summer months. They talked about the fun they were having playing shuffle board, swimming, playing tennis, and walking in the cool of the evenings. They spoke glowingly about their family home evening groups, the quietness of their sacrament meetings, and the rest they were enjoying after a lifetime of work.

Before long, the conversation took a subtle change of direction. They started to talk about their aches and pains. One would tell of the latest operation, describing in detail the operation and the convalescent period. Another would then describe their latest bout with the flu or a cold or whatever. A third transition occurred later in the evening. They started talking about plans for the future. We thought, considering the enthusiasm they were generating, that the possibility of serving a mission might surface. How disappointing to hear (in February) that the most anticipated event for the entire year was the Christmas light decorations they were in charge of for the next holiday season yet ten months away.

After we concluded a very lovely evening, we wondered if the Lord was expecting too much of people by asking them to get outside their comfort zone and serve missions. Surely these wonderful people had earned the right to relax and enjoy the fruits of their labors. Indeed they had! No one, the leaders of the Church included, would condemn them for taking that which was rightfully theirs. However, there is a much higher cause than self-service that awaits them if they are willing to consider it. That higher cause is following the Christ-like example of forgetting self in the service of others. In fact, the Savior taught a paradoxical precept: "He that findeth his life shall lose it: and he that loseth his life for my sake shall find it" (Matthew 10:39). By focusing on our own selfish needs, we atrophy spiritually, therefore making it more difficult to really find ourselves. By focusing outward, we grow spiritually to the point it is easy to really find ourselves.

To the Nephites the Savior taught: "Behold I am the light; I have set an example for you" (3 Nephi 18:16). Later in that same chapter, He gives the command: "Therefore, hold up your light that it may shine unto the world. Behold I am the light which ye shall hold up—that which ye have seen me do" (3 Nephi 18:24). If we are to follow the example of the Savior, can we legitimately take the final days of our mortal existence and relax? If the Savior had relaxed the last week of His mortal life, what difference would that have made to us? It is difficult to even comprehend the negative impact. No sacrament, no Atonement, no resurrection, virtually no nothing. The ancient Nephite prophet, Jacob, contemplated the impact of having no Atonement. He said:

> For as death hath passed upon all men, to fulfil the merciful plan of the great Creator, there must needs be a power of resurrection, and the resurrection must needs come unto man by reason of the fall; and the fall came by reason of transgression; and because man became fallen they were cut off from the presence of the Lord. Wherefore, it must needs be an infinite atonement—save it should be an infinite atonement this corruption could not put on incorruption. Wherefore, the first judgment which came upon man must needs have remained to an endless duration. And if so, this flesh must have laid down to rot and to crumble to its mother earth, to rise no more. O the wisdom of God, his mercy and grace! For behold, if the flesh should rise no more our spirits must become subject to that angel who fell from before the presence of the Eternal God, and became the devil, to rise no more. And our spirits must have become like unto him, and we become devils, angels to a devil, to be shut out from the presence of our God, and to remain with the father of lies, in misery, like unto himself. (2 Nephi 9:6–9)

It would be a bleak picture if the Savior had decided to take some much earned and needed rest rather than following through to the end. You may even be saying, "Well, He was the Savior and that was His assigned role. We are different." Perhaps the Savior was anticipating such a response. Before leaving the Nephites, He said: "Therefore, what manner of men ought ye to be? Verily I say unto you, even as I am" (3 Nephi 27:27). Surely, if He expects us to be like Him, it is possible to be so. It would be a cruel God to give commandments and expectations to His children without empowering them to accomplish what they were commanded.

What are the real comparisons and contrasts we should be making? Maybe to list just a few would be sufficient to demonstrate the contrast. Basking in the sun or baptizing souls unto Christ? Playing shuffle board or saving souls? Playing tennis or teaching the gospel of Jesus Christ? Relaxing in the sun or laboring in the Lord's vineyard? Enjoying family home evening with friends who have all been through the temple or struggling to teach and prepare families to enter the temple and receive the exalting ordinances? Driving aimlessly around enjoying the scenery or driving with purpose to locate our Father's lost sheep? Focusing on our own aches and pains or binding up the wounds of the weary, transgression-wounded souls? Hanging up Christmas lights or igniting the illuminating light of Christ in the lives of your investigators? Describing in detail your operations or participating as co-operators with the Master Healer in removing the sin caused cancer from the lives of good people?

Without wanting to make too big a deal of the differences, we would report that in the three years that we interfaced with the senior couples, and in the years following our mission experience, we have never had a conversation focus for more than a couple of minutes on aches and pains or operations. They are too eager to talk about the people they met, the experiences they enjoyed, and the challenges they overcame with the help of the Lord.

When people have too much time on their hands, they tend to focus on that which is of little eternal consequence. Someone told us many years ago a statement that changed our lives: "Small minds talk about people. Medium sized minds talk about things. Great minds talk about ideas!" We're not even sure it is totally true, but we are witnesses that there is a different feeling when gospel concepts predominate the discussion. Does the Spirit bear witness to gossip?

For an entire lifetime you have focused outward in an attempt to make a comfortable living for yourselves and your family. Great joy was the likely result. Why would you even consider changing the focus this late in the game? We always marveled at the young missionaries who would return home, abandon the truths they learned in the mission field, and then wonder why they didn't feel as happy as they did in the field.

We have seriously considered what we want to do during the "golden years." Are we going to fall prey to the worldly illusion of leisure, luxury, and no responsibility as being the utopia? That sounds very much like the large and spacious building in Lehi's vision of the tree of life.

A number of years ago while employed by the county surveyor, I noted that he was still working long past the retirement age. One day I asked him why he didn't retire since he had long since become financially independent. He told me that he had watched his friends retire. Within a year each of them had died. He didn't want to die and therefore decided that life needed to have some purpose or his fate would be the same as his friends. He passed away at the age of ninety-six. At the time I thought he was over-dramatizing the connection. Now I am not sure he wasn't exactly on target.

We were sent to earth with an assigned mission. We were promised sufficient time to complete the mission. When we lose focus on the purpose of life or lose momentum in accomplishing life's assigned mission, perhaps a loving Heavenly Father says, "I'd better get them out of their situation and into the spirit world where there is so much work to do that it will require the entire millennium to accomplish it."

There might be two ways of looking at that. Maybe we should slow down and prolong the completion of our assigned labors, therefore prolonging earth life. That seems rather contrary to the command of the Lord that we ought to be "anxiously engaged" in a good cause (see D&C 58:26–29). Perhaps a godlier approach would be to go to with all our might and complete what has been assigned so He can bless us with additional strength to complete yet more assignments. We may even be assigned to finish the assignments made by those who quit before they got to the end of the row.

Consider the First Presidency and Quorum of the Twelve. Because it is ever changing, it wouldn't be wise to calculate their average age. However, no faithful Latter-day Saint will argue that none of them are in retirement mode. Frequently we hear how younger members of the Quorum of the Seventy struggle to keep pace with the First Presidency and the Twelve. What makes the difference? Are they just supermen in bodies of clay like us? We would suspect that their vision, purpose, and continued activity in furthering the great cause of Zion literally renews them so they can fulfill their God-assigned missions.

Since God is no respecter of persons (see Acts 10:34), then He would be willing to do the same thing for each of His sons and daughters. Perhaps we are contributing to our own compromised health conditions by prematurely projecting ourselves into a state of retirement. That is not to say that we must continue on the job working until the day we die. However, working in the service of the Lord pays dividends that go far beyond the confines of mortality. Many of our retired friends (which obviously includes our senior couples) have concluded that they should have retired years earlier and gone full-time in the service of the Lord.

If you seriously ask, "How does God directly benefit from all of the work which He does?," you may come to a startling conclusion that virtually everything He does is for our benefit. In other words, He is totally outward focused. How can we truly become like Him if we insist on focusing on our own needs? The fact that a man does not use the priesthood to give himself a blessing ought to suggest how the Lord expects us to use our time and talents to bless others rather than just ourselves.

Sometimes it takes a huge dose of humility to admit that we have embarked on a path that is not totally consistent with the will of the Lord. Thankfully, the Lord has made provisions so we can back up and get it right the second time as long as we have not "sinned unto death" (D&C 64:7). There may yet be times in the future when you will be able to sit with your feet propped up and enjoy the life of leisure in the sun. But it could very well be after you have a wealth of experiences to talk about that you accumulated on your mission.

You may even find that the need is so great for you and your talents that you decide you still want to winter in a warmer climate but not where there are cities of other retired couples. There are so many little wards and branches scattered across the southern United States that would give anything to have you spend part of your year with them. True Christ-like service is not only contagious but, hopefully, terminal. Maybe even death doesn't cure us from our desire to serve as Christ did.

Before you rule out these options, why not serve your first mission as a couple and see what the Lord has in mind for you in the future? We are absolutely convinced, through our own experience, that missions bless everyone they touch. Therefore, we are bold in encouraging you to leave the life of ease and volunteer for the most difficult thing you have ever loved as a couple. The rewards are so great both in this world and in the world to come that we can't help but make an impassioned plea to do something for yourselves that you will be thankful for a long after time is counted no more. Missions are definitely God-inspired activities calculated to bless the missionaries as well as those who receive the gospel from them.

Chapter 25

A MISSION PRESIDENT'S DREAM COME TRUE

The calling of a mission president is unlike any other calling in the Church. So stated President Gordon B. Hinckley in the special week-long training for mission presidents and their wives. It is intense, demanding, never ending. It almost defies description. At times mission presidents feel like no one can understand their challenges. We are not saying this to solicit sympathy for those who are so called. We explain this so you will see that when a mission president gets missionary recommendation forms that include a senior couple, there is a new lease on life given to them.

There is something about having a couple assigned to the mission that revitalizes the president, his wife, and the entire mission staff. Why is it so? We're not sure. We just know that it was a reality in our mission every time it occurred. Much of what needs to be said has been alluded to in other chapters of this book. Our objective is not to be redundant, so we will confine our comments in this chapter to other areas of consideration.

Every year at Thanksgiving we would invite the senior couples to eat with us. They insisted (probably from years of habit) that they bring a portion of the meal. The meals almost defied description. Our children marveled at the spread that was laid before us. One of the traditions we have in our home is that before the meal starts each person takes a few seconds and tells about something he or she is really thankful for. As hungry as we all were, even the children sat spellbound as the senior couples shared some of their most sacred memories of thankfulness.

Not infrequently there were pauses while emotions were brought under control, as love for each other was expressed, thanksgiving for their families, for the gospel, for their health, for the privilege of serving missions, but mostly for the Lord. As they spoke so personally about their love for and relationship with the Savior, we silently gave thanks to our Heavenly Father that our children had the privilege of participating in such a sacred moment. There was never any hint of impatience by our children, although the tradition often took quite some time to complete.

The couples blessed our family in ways that they will never know. They were the grandparents we had left behind. They were the role models for our children during the very formative years while we were separated from our extended family. Their spirits kindled in us a determination to be more like them. If we, as mission president, ever considered getting discouraged (yes, even mission presidents struggle), a single meeting with the senior couples raised our spirits above the impossibility of the task required of us. We will be forever grateful to the senior couples for the impact they had on our lives.

Because my father died when I was very young, I look at the experiences we shared with the senior couples as the Lord's way of compensating me for the good times I missed out on because I didn't have a father in mortality. I am confident that none of the senior couples were ever aware of how much I enjoyed listening to them talk, joke with each other, and tease Sister Bott and me while sharing a meal or enjoying a couple's conference.

Senior couples have a way about them that is instructive even for mission presidents. They are very unpretentious. They go about doing good without ever expecting to receive public recognition. Often the young missionaries want to be recognized for the good works they do. The senior couples were generally just the opposite. They wanted to avoid the limelight as much as possible. Here were truly great people who deferred reference to their greatness and preferred praising others with far less accomplishments. Because many couples were so modest about their own accomplishments, it was difficult to "get the goods" on them for our Christmas socials. It was only by their good-natured willingness to "snitch" on the other couples that we were really able to find out much about them.

Senior couples were problem solvers. It wasn't so much what they said or did as much as it was their presence that disarmed so many potentially explosive situations. We would marvel how much smoother the mission ran when a senior couple was in a certain zone. As usual, they were totally unaware of the impact they had because they didn't have the opportunity to see the entire mission. We always felt a little bad when the couples would want us to have lunch with them and we couldn't because of interviews or other pressing matters. They were always so thoughtful. However, they were counterproductive to our weight-control plan. We have never eaten so much good food as we did when we would dine with the couples.

Even in zone conference, the senior couples had a moderating influence. Being a teacher by profession, I would tend to forget that the mind can only absorb as much as the seat can endure. The senior couples were the only ones brave enough to raise their hand in the middle of some doctrinal discourse and suggest we take a break since we had been meeting for four straight hours. I always felt a little embarrassed that I wasn't sensitive enough to consider their needs without having to be reminded. We enjoyed some good-natured ribbing over issues where I should have been more attentive.

Couples could be counted on in a pinch. If a missionary came in at a time other than the regular transfer, the couples were willing to meet them at the airport and entertain them until we could arrange to be back for our orientation interview. If a missionary had to leave at an odd time that conflicted with other items on our pressing agenda, the senior couples were always gracious to offer to take them to the airport and see them off. Just those little things make all the difference in the world. It is frustrating to be scheduled to be in two or three places at once with no possibility of making all of the appointments. Very often our salvation was in the substitute service the senior couples provided until we could arrive.

Senior couples were like having multiple counselors. They were probably unaware how many times we would drop in just to chat when we needed someone with a fresh, seasoned, new approach to a nagging problem. Often their proposed solutions were just far enough off the mark that they were hilarious. If we had followed through on some of their suggestions, the Lord would have had an increase in the size of the missionary force in the spirit world! After making their harsh suggestion, we would all laugh. Conditions didn't seem quite so impossible after a good session of laughter. They will likely never know how many times we just needed someone to share a problem with who was mature enough not to fall to pieces at the complexity of the problem. We didn't share confidential information with them, but the principles they had learned over many years often opened our minds to more options for possible solutions.

Senior couples often tried to be the parents we were separated from. Because we were the ages of many of their children, they sort of felt it their responsibility to at least tell us to slow down and take better care of ourselves. Although slowing down really wasn't an option, the memories of them caring about our health was comforting. They tried, without success, to baby us. Occasionally a plate of cookies, a pie, or some homemade soup would find its way to the mission home just when we were returning from a grueling week of zone conferences. We were probably not as appreciative as we should have been in letting them know what their acts of kindness did for our spirits. In retrospect, I should have done much more to express our love and appreciation to the senior couples for literally saving our lives in so many different ways.

Senior elders were available when my counselors were not to participate with me in Church disciplinary councils. Although not a frequent occurrence, it was comforting to know that I had a support system of unparalleled experience to help me decide some delicate issues. To call on two brethren who had served as bishops, members of stake presidencies, on high councils as helps during a disciplinary council distributed the weight of the burden that was compounded by so many other factors they did not have to know. Their clear thinking and wealth of past experience made a difficult situation not only manageable but enjoyable for all involved.

Senior couples demonstrated maturity and tact when they would see that a missionary or member had cornered one or both of us at a meeting or conference. They would often come and divert the person's attention or take them on a walk so we could continue with our assigned duties without appearing rude or uncaring. Too many times to count, the senior couples would come to our rescue. Everyone was satisfied and no one got the idea we didn't care about them or have time for them. Occasionally we would overhear a conversation between a couple and a particularly insensitive missionary as they taught them about consideration and tact. Although, rightly we should have done the teaching, the demands of the office kept us jumping all the time. Therefore, some of the little, fine tuning, and polishing points were performed by couples.

Without being pushy or presumptuous the couples would go about identifying what needed to be done and just do it. We never had to ask, we were never let down, and we were never disappointed when the couples were given an assignment. If it has been awhile since you have worked with teenagers, you might be in for a shock. Many have successfully evaded the learning of the finer points of human relationships. Manners, by some, are viewed as old-fashioned and not necessary. Rules of etiquette were often strange and unheard of by the younger missionaries. It was humorous and gratifying to watch the senior couples take the younger missionaries to task at a Christmas banquet for using the table cloth to wipe their hands. Before long we could notice a definite difference in their behavior. We loved watching the couples refine the missionaries.

The comforting influence of a senior couple on a young missionary who had just learned of the separation of his parents was crucial until we could arrive. Their continued follow up after we had done all we could do was necessary to help him stabilize in a very difficult situation. We knew we could count on the senior couples holding things together until we could arrive, no matter what the problems were. We were never disappointed.

It was generally the senior couples who would be thoughtful enough to send a thank you card and note after a zone conference, or a Christmas meal, or at the conclusion of their mission. We recognized the excitement of the young missionaries when they would depart and really didn't expect them to express any appreciation. A few did. But the couples were more expressive of their appreciation. Several times we thought about the experience of the Savior with the ten lepers who were cleansed but only one returned to express appreciation. Perhaps learning to express appreciation is something that happens with the passage of years.

The influence of the senior couples continues to bless our lives. Not just in the memories we have of shared times, but in the continued association we have with them. The young missionaries return home, go off to school, get married, and start their lives—all of which are very desirable. They don't have time to keep in close contact with their mission president, although the president and wife will always hold a special place in their hearts. However, the senior couples return from their missions and resume their lives. Therefore, they seem to have more time and interest in keeping our relationship alive. What a joy it was to look at the congregation during our homecoming and see an entire section of the chapel filled with senior couples. We would suspect that a few couple's conferences in the eternal world would not be out of order.

There are so many other ways that couples impact a mission president's life. Scattered throughout this book are references to just some of the ways you enrich a mission. Rather than continuing the list, we want to say that we want to be the one leper who returns to the Savior and expresses our eternal thanks for the privilege we had of working with the senior couples. The bonds of love and mutual respect will never end. Our task would have been impossible and unbearable had it not been for the influence and help of our beloved senior couples.

Chapter 26

LOVING THE PEOPLE

All missionaries, including couples, face homesickness when they arrive in the mission field. The newness of the surroundings, the leaving of home and loved ones, the strangeness of the routine of daily missionary life, almost everything contributes to a feeling that happens sometime during the first few months. It is best verbalized by a statement we heard time and again from the young missionaries: "President, I don't think I'm cut out to be a missionary! I want to go home!" It was serious to them, so we tried not to smile or laugh. We would explain that everyone felt the same way at times during their mission. We tried to help them through the experience as quickly and painlessly as possible. Almost always, they thought they were the only one who ever felt that way.

One particular young man was really homesick. He even had his bags packed and was insistent that he return home. We decided to hold a district meeting before he left. We invited our two assistants, the most revered young missionaries in the field, and his zone leader to attend. The district leader conducted the meeting, and the district members (including the homesick elder) were there. We prearranged the seating so he was on the far left side of a semi-circle. Sister Bott and I were sitting in front of the semi-circle of missionaries. We started at the far right and had each elder and sister tell about their struggle to adjust. The further we went around the circle, each recounting his or her story, the more attention the homesick elder gave.

Each missionary seemed to have a story that was just a little better or funnier than the one before. This young elder's role model (one of our assistants) was sitting adjacent to him. As this noble elder shared his story, the whole group erupted into laughter as he explained how he felt isolated and alone. He was sure he was the only one who had ever experienced these feelings. He had called the mission president (our predecessor) and requested a ticket home.

When the assistant finished, we turned to the homesick elder. He said, "President, you have made your point. I'll be okay." Then, turning to his companion, he said, "Why didn't you tell me you'd had these same feelings? I thought I was the only one!"

The meeting ended with another round of laughter. As we parted, the zone leader remained behind. That was always a sign that they wanted to talk. I pulled him aside and asked if everything was all right. He started to cry. I put my arm around his shoulder and asked what the trouble was. He reminded me of something I knew already. "President, I'm due to be released this transfer. Please don't make me go home! I don't want to leave. I love the work, I love the people, I love my companion, I love the gospel, and I love the Lord and I don't want to lose what I have here!"

His pleading voice reminded me that almost all really good missionaries, especially senior couples, do not want to leave when their missions are complete. It happened so frequently that we called it "reverse homesickness." Others have labeled it "mission homesickness." No matter what term you use to describe it, it is real and more difficult to overcome than regular homesickness.

You know you will be spending the rest of your lives with your families. All of the holidays, birthdays, special days, reunions, and so on will be with those you thought you could never leave for even a year or two. Now the realization hits that you are going to be leaving people you have learned to love as much—sometimes even more—than your own family. The chances of you seeing them again is remote. The likelihood that you will spend much time with them is almost an impossibility. You know that when you leave, you probably won't see them again in this life.

The experience you will have is not unique. When the Apostle Paul realized that he would no longer be free to revisit the beloved

Saints he had sacrificed his life for, he informed them: "And now, behold, I know that ye all, among whom I have gone preaching the kingdom of God, shall see my face no more" (Acts 20:25). The reaction of the people has not changed in almost two thousand years. They said: "And when he had thus spoken, he kneeled down, and prayed with them all. And they all wept sore, and fell on Paul's neck, and kissed him, Sorrowing most of all for the words which he spake, that they should see his face no more. And they accompanied him unto the ship" (Acts 20:36–38).

Why is there such a bond that develops between missionaries and the converts? Perhaps Elder L. Tom Perry identifies part of the reason: "One couple then reported, as they concluded their mission, that in the final testimony meeting these words were spoken of them: "Dear elder and sister, you just can't imagine what our life was like before you came."[1] Sometimes the missionary is so engrossed in helping the family understand the gospel that they fail to recognize the night and day difference between what the family was like before and what they are like now.

Missionaries are prone to look beyond the exterior and see into the hearts of the people. Since they are looking for the "golden contacts," they often overlook the very telestial exterior. Although missionaries may not notice the monumental changes, the family does. They compare the level of happiness they enjoyed as family, the sense of fulfillment they had, and the direction their lives were taking before and are often overwhelmed at the differences.

Why do you love your children and grandchildren so much? One possible answer is that you sacrificed everything for them. Your needs came after theirs. Purchasing things you wanted was often postponed to buy something they wanted. You virtually gave your lives for them and thus the Christ-like love developed. Even more pointedly than with your family, you will be literally sacrificing your lives for these wonderful people. Whereas your family developed over many years, these people you have been instrumental in converting have been "born again" almost overnight.

When a person is born, they come into the world as a baby. Mother and Father have to care for the baby's every need or he or she will physically perish. When a person is "born again," he also comes into the kingdom of God as a little child. If his spiritual needs are not met on a daily basis, he will die, not because he is not a good person but because the caregivers (the members of the Church) are not as attentive as they need to be. One of President Hinckley's greatest concerns was the number of new converts who fall away after their baptism. Members are busy. That really isn't intended as an excuse for them but more as an explanation. Senior missionaries often become the lifesaving link for the new member with the Church.

Just as your children looked to you for their very existence, so the new members will look to you for their spiritual life. As you nurture them through the difficult first months when their families, friends, former church members, and ministers are all trying to help them "see the error of their ways," they really need your help. As they conform their lives to the expectations of the gospel, the Spirit starts to work with them in a miraculous way. You see them change and grow from day to day. As you point out their progress, they begin to take courage and develop the hope that they really can make it to the celestial kingdom.

Then comes the day when they are prepared to enter the temple. As they kneel around the sacred altar, possibly with you acting as their escorts, the reward comes vividly to your minds. If it hadn't been for your influence, they likely never would be enjoying the ecstasy of the moment. You have literally been their mortal saviors. As their children are ushered into the sealing room, all dressed in white, you are sure that you have died and gone to heaven. Nothing could be as sublime as what you are experiencing. In fact, nothing can because you are experiencing true charity—the pure love of Christ.

What seemed like such a long way away the day you arrived in the mission field is now approaching with frightening rapidity—your release date. You are a little different from the younger missionaries. If you plead enough and make a big enough fuss, the president can get permission from Salt Lake City to extend your mission. The younger missionaries are not so fortunate. The president only has the latitude of extending or shortening their missions by thirty days to accommodate the needs of the mission. However, for most of you, the departure date set by the Church will be the day you return home.

Terror now fills your souls, not because of the fear of what comes next but because you are very excited about being reunited with your families. The terror comes with the realization that you are closing a chapter on your life that will likely never be opened again. Many couples reported that they had been praying fervently to the Lord to slow down the clock. But, alas, the last six months of your mission passes five times as quickly as the first six months.

As your beloved members and investigators realize that you will be leaving soon, they do something cruel—they start to mourn your departure. They bring you gifts and mementos so you won't forget them. They write you notes and letters of love and appreciation. They all want to pose with you for multiple pictures. They want you to visit and give just one more family home evening lesson. They want just one more picnic in the park, one more visit to a museum, one more trip to the national forest, one more, one more, one more. It is not physically possible to satisfy everyone's wishes, and sometimes feelings are hurt when you have to tell them "no."

Then comes the fateful day. The mission president's secretary calls and informs you of the time of your exit interview. If you drove to the mission field, you realize the virtual impossibility of getting everything into the car that you have accumulated. If you flew to the mission, you have discovered that shipping things home is prohibitively expensive. What to do? We can't tell you! The little cardboard castle that a favored Primary child made for you must go home with you—no matter what the cost! The wall hanging the grateful mother made for you after her family was sealed in the temple is an absolute must. The stack of papers the Primary children colored as a farewell gift could not possibly be left behind. So, what do you do? As you sort through each item, you see that your hearts are intertwined in that memento to the point that it must be taken.

Many couples end up leaving their own clothes and personal belongings so they can take their memories. Others are willing to "mortgage the farm" to have everything shipped home. About the time you have everything packed and there is scarcely room enough for the two of you to fit in the car, the other senior couples will drop by with a "love basket" of food—just a little something to tide you over on your return trip. The members, fearing that you will not have enough to eat, will bring more food. Fear not, you will not be the first couple who have driven away from your apartment, drowning in tears and holding baskets of food on your laps and not being able to see out the rear view mirror.

The experience at the mission home only compounds the emotional problems you are now experiencing. The mission president and wife embrace you warmly and tell you how much they love you and how grateful they are for the service you have rendered. They are so sincere that you know they are speaking from the heart. Even the hard-hearted president often sheds tears as he tells you how they will miss you.

Then comes the exit interview. Each of you is asked to report, in summary form, what you have gained from your mission. By this time, you will likely be so emotionally drained that you're not at all sure you can survive a mental review. Often the interview with the senior couples takes much longer than with the younger missionaries. As you each reflect over the lessons you have learned, the people you have met, the spiritual experiences you have enjoyed, the trials you have endured, the friends you have made, the lives you have seen changed, and the testimonies you have seen strengthened—yours and others—the Spirit comes into your heart with such power that you know your heart will break.

Some of the most spiritual experiences we had as mission president were the exit interviews with our senior couples. It seemed at times that the Savior Himself must have been right there with us. Scripturally speaking, He was! "Verily, verily, I say unto you, as I said unto my disciples, where two or three are gathered together in my name, as touching one thing, behold, there will I be in the midst of them—even so am I in the midst of you" (D&C 6:32). Anyone who has been through one of those exit interviews will know of a surety that what the Lord promised, He also fulfilled. Those were wonderful experiences.

At the conclusion of the interview you all kneel together. The mission president, acting as voice during the prayer, asks Heavenly Father for a manifestation to you signifying the Lord's acceptance of your labors while in the mission field. If you weren't overwhelmed before, you likely will be at this time. We have witnessed direct and profound revelation given to senior couples signifying the Lord's acceptance of their missions. As you listen to the blessing being pronounced under the influence of the Spirit, you again realize that a mission was not really a sacrifice at all. It was a blessing without being in disguise.

You might ask, "Isn't there a cure or a way to avoid this reverse homesickness?" If there is, we have never discovered it. Your beloved Saints may as well rip out your hearts and hand them to you on a platter. Thankfully it is not fatal—usually! Although you will exit the mission field with a broken heart, it will heal. Although you are sure you will never sense joy like you did during those final days, you will when you meet your family. Even if you are confident that nothing will equal a mission—you are right, nothing will. Sorry! That's just the way the Lord seems to have designed the program.

So how do you prepare for this traumatic experience? You don't. It is just one of those rites of passage that happens to all good missionaries. We wish we could be there to experience this with you. Unfortunately, that level of spiritual highs would probably burn us out before long. We are so appreciative to the Lord for the opportunities He afforded us to participate with the senior couples and younger missionaries in this very sacred experience. Those who never serve will never experience (in this life) such an experience. Don't short change yourselves. Start the wheels rolling now to ensure that you don't miss out on this transcendent spiritual experience.

NOTE

1. L. Tom Perry, *Ensign*, May 1984, 80.

Chapter 27
CAPSTONE OF A LIFE OF SERVICE

As you reflect on your lives of service to family, Church, and the community, how do you intend on tying all the loose ends together? Sometimes it is difficult to identify a single event that seemed to make sense out of everything else that has happened. It is an acknowledged fact that you will not live in mortality forever. If you have been members of the Church for very many years, you have likely come to the realization that without the gospel your lives and everything in them would be drastically different. Your knowledge of the great plan of salvation answers the major questions puzzling the world: Where did I come from? What is the purpose of life? Where do I go following death?

A self-proclaimed atheist was on a talk show not too long ago espousing his ideas about life's meaning. He was an educated man, by the standards of the world, and could articulate very well his distorted understanding of life. An overwhelming sense of gratitude engulfed me as I listened to his story and realized that he knew nothing of the joy that comes from having a firm testimony that God is at the helm and that there really is purpose to mortality. As the show's host made fun of some of his comments, and as he responded by saying there is no physical proof of the existence of God, I realized that he had lived longer than I have and refused to experience the promptings of the Spirit, which are more sure than physical evidence that there is a God and that He really is our father.

That talk show experience set my mind to thinking about how much I know that I take for granted and how badly the world needs the information that brings joy and satisfaction to my soul constantly. In Lehi's final counsel to his sons, just prior to his passing from mortality, he explained: "Wherefore, how great the importance to make these things known unto the inhabitants of the earth, that they may know that there is no flesh that can dwell in the presence of God, save it be through the merits, and mercy, and grace of the Holy Messiah, who layeth down his life according to the flesh, and taketh it again by the power of the Spirit, that he may bring to pass the resurrection of the dead, being the first that should rise" (2 Nephi 2:8).

How could I consider sitting comfortably in my armchair, enjoying the thoughts and blessings of eternal life, while billions of my brothers and sisters are perishing without even a correct knowledge of God? Perhaps you might consider making the capstone of your life to share what you have and enjoy with those who, for reasons known only to God, were not born with the same privileges.

As you strip away, one at a time, the influences the gospel has in your lives, it won't take long before you realize that your entire spiritual and physical life would resemble a skeleton void of skin, muscle, or vital organs. No one who still enjoys the presence of the Spirit would consider exchanging the richness of life we now enjoy for the poverty-stricken life without the gospel. While it is true that those who have never experienced the gospel may not know what they are missing, it is not true that there isn't a void in their lives.

Sometimes we wonder out loud what our reception will be in the spirit world following mortality if we neglect the prophet's call to share what we have with others. Elder David B. Haight re-emphasized the urgent pleas of Presidents Kimball and Benson for more couples: "For some time we have been encouraging qualified mature couples to serve full-time missions. President Kimball and President Benson have stated that the goal of physically able couples and some women who may now be single is to serve a mission.

The need remains. Indeed, the requests from mission presidents for more—many more—couples are becoming more pressing."[1]

This entire book has been dedicated to helping you gain a broader vision of what the needs are throughout the world and how you can help meet those needs. The book was never intended to portray a mission as an easy task. It would not be a true representation to show missions as free of sacrifices and heartaches. It would be truthful to show that missions are the greatest thing you could do with the remaining healthy years of your lives.

Could we fantasize a little for a moment? You will recall the Lord's explanation to Joseph Smith and the early brethren of this dispensation: "Wherefore, you are called to cry repentance unto this people. And if it so be that you should labor all your days in crying repentance unto this people, and bring, save it be one soul unto me, how great shall be your joy with him in the kingdom of my Father! And now, if your joy will be great with one soul that you have brought unto me into the kingdom of my Father, how great will be your joy if you should bring many souls unto me!" (D&C 18:14–16).

Just how great will our joy be? Can you envision a time in the distant eternities when you and your spouse have been crowned with celestial exaltation? You may have been engaged for some time in the process of creating and peopling worlds. All of the joy that our Father promised we would enjoy is now ours. Our resurrected children, grandchildren, and all of our posterity are available to visit at our pleasure. The challenges of administering countless worlds does not seem difficult at all since you have gained all knowledge and all power. With your unlimited capacity, the two of you are beginning to understand what the prophets spoke of while you were yet in mortality.

While surveying your endless creations, a call comes on your celestial cellular phone. The voice on the other end asks if you have time for a brief visit. Since time is not counted anymore, you extend the invitation for them to come. In an instant two glorious, resurrected, exalted beings are at your side. They fall at your feet in a gesture of supreme appreciation. As you bid them arise you recognize them as a couple you taught while on your mission just before the end of your mortal test. They embrace you and profusely thank you for sharing the gospel with them, which enabled them to enjoy the remainder of their mortal lives and have the necessary ordinances performed that opened to them the gates leading to the highest degree of the celestial kingdom.

They acknowledge that without your willingness to sacrifice your well-earned comforts, they may have been deprived during mortality from all the blessings the gospel brings. Then, with a grand gesture of the sweeping of his arm, your friend opens to your eternal vision a panorama of worlds without numbers. Your infinite abilities enable the two of you to see endless billions of sons and daughters who have been born to this couple, in varying stages of eternal progression. With tears in their eyes they turn to you and say, "All of these creations and children owe their opportunities for eternal life to you. Without your being saviors on Mount Zion for us, we could not have enjoyed these eternal blessings."

Then it begins to dawn on you why the Lord said that laboring all your days with the result of bringing a single soul unto Him in the kingdom of His Father would result in eternities of joy with them in the celestial kingdom. It wasn't just the one little boy that you baptized during your mission that really counted. It was the eternal potential of each individual you influenced that really made the difference.

Perhaps our imaginations have run a little out of control—or have they? Because we are required to learn to live by faith, the veil between us and our pre-earth life has kept us from seeing the full eternal implications of our actions. The nearer we approach perfection, the clearer our views become and the more inclined we are to accept the counsel of our living prophets and participate with them in fulfilling our Father's grand objective for us.

The Prophet Joseph Smith explained how expansive our vision would have to be in order to help guide our Father's children back to His divine presence. "Thy mind, O man! if thou wilt lead a soul unto salvation, must stretch as high as the utmost heavens, and search into and contemplate the darkest abyss, and the broad expanse of eternity—thou must commune with God. How much more dignified and noble are the thoughts of God, than the vain imaginations of the human heart! None but fools will trifle with the souls of men."[2]

Have we become so narrow in our thinking that we fail to grasp the essential nature of our total efforts to bring about the immortality and eternal life of ourselves, our families, and our other brothers and sisters who are not yet members of the Church?

Over your lifetime the two of you have gained many wonderful friends and associates. As you approach the last leg of your mortal experience, you can see how much richer your lives are because of those friends. Most retired couples have a sufficiently large circle of friends that they seldom venture out into untried areas. Imagine what a mission would do to change that. You will meet hundreds of new friends. Your old friends will still be there doing what they have always done. Your new friends will bring vitality, youthfulness, and excitement into your lives which you may have thought had disappeared forever.

Your old friends were friends because of beliefs and interests that you shared in common. Your new friends will be the same. The people you meet in the mission field will bring a dimension of eternity to your relationship. With their focus on the next life, you will find that you are thinking, talking, reading, discussing, and dreaming about eternity far more than you ever did at home. When the Lord is not far from the thoughts and the intents of your heart, it is much easier to stay focused and enthused about living all of the commandments.

One of the great fears of the young missionaries was that they might return home and fall back into pre-mission ways. We urged them to continue to study, pray, and work to maintain their spiritual cutting edge. One of the fears many couples have is that they will lose their spiritual cutting edge as they get older.

Consider the Relief Society and elders quorum meetings where you attend. It isn't right, but it is the way things often turn out that the current leaders look at the senior couples as "over the hill" and incapable of carrying heavy burdens in the local wards. That is definitely not the case in the mission field. In fact, just the opposite is generally true. In the mission field many couples feel overwhelmed at the trust the leaders put in them. They feel anything but unneeded.

With the new focus on using you to the maximum, it only takes a few minutes until the Spirit is pumping you up so you will be equal to the tasks required of you. If your home ward leaders have put you on the shelf as a spiritual relic, how about joining the army of very young senior couples who have discovered a new lease on life through extended Church service?

The capstone then becomes like a three-cornered hat. First you are sharing the life-giving insights you may have come to consider as common place, with a people who are dying to understand how you can possibly have been married fifty years and still love each other. As you share with them your trade secrets, they will not only be able to find joy in this life but eternal life in the world to come. You have literally become saviors on Mount Zion in helping them understand and perform those essential ordinances prerequisite to gaining eternal life.

Second, you will have expanded your pool of acquaintances beyond anything you now enjoy. These friends will hold you in such high esteem it may be a temptation to believe everything good they say about you. There is a distinct advantage to these friends over your old friends with whom you have grown up and old with over the years. These new friends have only seen you at your celestial best. If you had weaknesses and faults in the past, these people will never know of them. You are near perfect in their eyes. Perhaps that is why so many couples loved to be around their newly earned friends even more than the old ones.

Third, you will extend your usability in the Church beyond the time when most seniors are put out to pasture. Working with Primary, Young Men, Young Women, Sunday School, Relief Society, and priesthood leaders will make you feel young again. It will not be unusual to feel thirty years younger while you are serving a mission. While your friends at home may be sleeping through their meetings, you will be teaching them or coaching others how to teach them. Whereas at home the bishop would likely never call you to work with the younger children, in the mission field you can directly influence members and non-members of all ages.

Somebody forgot to tell our senior couples that they were too old to serve. It was a marvel to watch the difference between the senior missionary couples and those senior couples who were regular members of the local units. The local senior couples would refuse to acknowledge that they were younger than our senior missionary couples. It just isn't a good thing to have someone twenty to thirty years your senior make you look like an old retired couple.

The capstone is there for you to place on your lives. Forever you will be grateful that your final interview with the Savior will be non-threatening when He asks, "Did you serve a mission at the end of your lives, as I commanded you?" What a thrill to be able to take each other by the hand and confidently answer, "We actually served four missions after retirement age." Imagine how you'll feel when the Savior says, "Well done, thou good and faithful servant: thou hast been faithful over a few things, I will make thee ruler over many things: enter thou into the joy of thy lord" (Matthew 25:21).

NOTES

1. David B. Haight, *Ensign*, November 1988, 83.
2. *Teachings of the Prophet Joseph Smith*, 137.

Chapter 28

LOOKING AHEAD: VIRTUAL MISSIONS

For those who feel they can't serve full-time missions away from home at this time, there are options that are just beginning to emerge. Because of the recent pandemic, travel is restricted to some areas of the world. As a result, people are being required to devise creative ways of living their lives. Educational institutions have figured out how to teach classes over the internet. Doctors have found ways of consulting with their patients without requiring a face-to-face visit. Financial institutions have figured out how to transact business dealings via internet. Companies have devised way of having employees work from home, and the list goes on.

Because we belong to a dynamic kingdom, the Church will continue to expand the way we serve missions. Consider how the Church has adapted to the pandemic to enable members to conduct meetings without congregating in large groups. Pardon a personal example as I dream with you about future possibilities.

When the pandemic hit in March of 2020, we had just submitted our papers for a third couple mission—hopefully to be assigned to Sydney, Australia, where we served our second mission. Travel restrictions stopped us, like everyone else, from fulfilling our dream. That, however didn't prevent us from "serving a mission." We have been teaching a weekly Pathway institute class from our home in

Orem, Utah, to the class with members scattered over the eastern part of Australia. The inconvenience is that there is an eight-hour time difference. So, their "Wednesday at 6:00 a.m." is our "Tuesday at 2:00 p.m." They don't seem to mind and neither do we. Also, we have been doing "pastoral counseling" (non-professional) with a couple in New Zealand and one in Australia, and giving lectures at their educational conferences. We are working with the family services director in localizing a manual for self-resilience.

All of the above is with the permission of our local priesthood leaders and according to our schedule. We have the advantage of staying at home (enjoying the grandchildren) and still serving. We are loving this kind of a mission!

Before long is it not unlikely that the Church will capitalize on what the world has been forced to learn because of the disruption of the pandemic. There are virtually thousands and tens of thousands of senior couples who for one reason or another (health, finances, family, and so on) do not feel free to leave home to serve. They would willingly spend time each week helping and advising others around the globe from the comfort of their own homes using the amazing technology currently available, capitalizing on their years of experience, and teaching new or inexperienced members what is second nature to them.

To name just a few opportunities that could soon become available: retired educators, business professionals and owners, farmers, ranchers, electricians, construction workers, health workers, lawyers, doctors, financial experts, engineers, and so on. Consider the financial savings of serving from home and the diminished family impact that such a mission might have. The Church will always need couple missionaries who are willing and able to leave home to serve abroad, but this could open opportunities to serve to a currently untapped resource of willing missionaries.

Now to expand the pool of potential missionaries, consider the almost limitless pool of bishops, high councilors, stake presidents, mission presidents, area authority Seventies, stake and ward Relief Society leaders, and Young Women and Primary leaders who have served faithfully but, in due time have been released—too often to be put on the shelf of non-required leaders as younger men and women are called to positions they once held. Here are people with experience that cannot be totally contained in a church manual. How the developing wards and branches could benefit from their lifetime of service.

Almost instantly the potential missionary force could be increased from tens of thousands to hundreds of thousands. But with unlimited possibilities, options to serve aren't finished yet. As of the writing of this book, the Church does not call single senior brethren on missions. These are men who have faithfully served all their lives but are either widowed, have spouses with health problems, or are compromised themselves health-wise to where they are functional but not sufficiently healthy to leave home and serve full-time. These men have accumulated, through their service, the "wisdom of the aged." They are the very ones who Joseph Smith said were the key to get along in any important matter: "The way to get along in any important matter is to gather unto yourselves wise men, experienced and aged men, to assist in council in all times of trouble. Handsome men are not apt to be wise and strong-minded men; but the strength of a strong-minded man will generally create course features, like the rough, strong bough of the oak. You will always discover in the first glance of a man, in the outlines of his features something of his mind."[1]

Rather than spending endless hours on the golf course (not to criticize those who do for taking time to enjoy the golden years) I am confident that any one of them would willingly devote several hours a week to further the cause of Zion. What if each new convert could be linked to a senior missionary serving from home to help them stay involved and grow in the Church? What if our great temple officiators could shepherd new (and old) members as they prepare to enter or re-enter the temple? Could we decrease the number of those who "come in the front door and out the back"?

Just one more dream as we speculate on the limitless opportunities for those who are willing to serve in the future. Consider the number of women who were faced with the decision to serve a mission or get married. They, having chosen the latter, have always wanted to serve but now have children at home and the prospect of being able to serve with their husbands may be decades away. Yet the desire is there. Many are well educated but all are experienced in meeting the challenges of motherhood and negotiating the rapids of marital challenges. Many of them would gladly take a few hours a week to advise, counsel, teach, or minister to someone in need of help.

Now the potential missionary force has increased from hundreds of thousands to virtually millions of missionaries. Working through the priesthood channels of area presidencies working with local leaders, and coordinating the massive effort through Salt Lake, there is no reason why, as a Church, we can't fulfil President David O. McKay's charge: "Every member a missionary."

Are these possibilities realistic? Absolutely! We belong to a living, dynamic Church. We believe that "God will yet reveal many great and important things pertaining to the Kingdom of God" (Articles of Faith 1:9). Is this the final word that is likely to come from the Lord concerning senior missionaries? Experience has proven that we can expect a flood of new directives as we close in on the final days preceding the Second Coming of the Lord. All we wait for is direction from the Lord through His chosen leaders—keep your eyes on the living prophets.

NOTE

1. *Teachings of the Prophet Joseph Smith*, 299.

Chapter 29

LIVING LIFE IN CRESCENDO

After all has been said there remains but one question that each must answer for himself. What will be my final report when, in the not-too-distant-future, I stand to account for my earthly experience? Many athletic teams have suffered a common problem; they "peaked" too early in the season. When it came time to play in the finals, they were past their prime, and many who had been front runners earlier in the season failed to make the play-offs. What happened? Was it lack of talent? Obviously not, they had led the pack earlier in the season. Perhaps if we could assess the exact cause of their premature peaking, we could become very wealthy people. No matter what the cause, the results are always disappointment and regret.

Must life be lived like that? Can we live so that we end on an all-time high? Elder Brigham H. Roberts said of the Prophet Joseph Smith:

> The Prophet lived his life in crescendo. From small beginnings, it rose in breadth and power as he neared its close. As a teacher he reached the climax of his career in this discourse [King Follet Discourse]. After it there was but one thing more he could do—seal his testimony with his blood. This he did less than three months later. Such is not the manner of life of false prophets.[1]

Not once but many, many times we witnessed the following scene: Young children gathered around a senior couple, clinging to their legs, pleading for them to stay. Tears streamed down the little faces as the made statements such as, "Please don't leave us. We can't live without you. We love you. You are the best thing that ever happened to us." Although those statements often did come from the children, it was actually the adults whom we are quoting.

Several couples had served faithfully for the prescribed one-year mission. They were eager to return home to their family, friends, properties, and businesses. After the tearful farewells, they departed the mission. Within a month they called and asked if they could return to the mission. We were delighted to welcome them back on the Lord's first team. During the re-entry interviews we would ask about their change of heart. Through their own tears they had recounted how they had returned home, and their families had hovered around them for a few days to a couple of weeks. Then life returned to normal. Children and grandchildren came over weekly or even less frequently. Friends had things they had to do. As they sat in their comfortable homes, they realized that they weren't really as needed at home as they were in the mission field. Looking at each other over the breakfast table, they had admitted the inevitable—their mission was not complete. Many came back for another six months; some came for a year. Others went home, put their affairs in order, and signed up for another mission.

Many of our couples were serving their second, third, and fourth missions. They had learned to live life in crescendo. To say that serving a mission was easy would not be a true statement. Many reported that considering their diminished health and stamina, it was the most difficult task they had ever undertaken. When asked why they subjected themselves to the rigors of missionary work even though they had multiple aches and pains, they looked at us with rather surprised looks. "Why, President, we thought you, of all people, would understand! This is the Lord's work. We are honored to be part of it. What difference does a few aches and pains make? We would have them at home! The rewards of being on a mission so far outweigh the inconveniences, that it isn't even a question what to do when an honest comparison is made!"

It was always fun to be put in our place by the senior couples. They were virtually old enough to be our parents, and yet they treated us with love and respect. It was difficult to get after them when they would smile so lovingly and agree with our directives and then quietly go about doing what their age and wisdom dictated was the right course of action. We wondered at times who really ran the mission. We readily concede that without the help of the senior couples, our task as mission president would have been infinitely more difficult.

In reviewing the multitude of senior couples we have been blessed to know, it is nearly impossible to find a couple who regrets going on a mission. On the other hand, the expressions of appreciation, fulfillment, love, joy, and thanksgiving expressed by those who have served have made my wife and me anxious to get out and serve again.

In keeping with the title of this chapter, could we review your progress to this point? Rather than start with your mortal birth, let's go back to a time long before there was life on earth. There, a loving Father and Mother provided spirit bodies for your intelligence. Although not yet in possession of a physical body, you had a spirit body that resembled our Heavenly Parents. Their objective from that very beginning was to help us develop into what they had become. The Prophet Joseph Smith clarified God's methodology in helping us develop by stating:

> The first principles of man are self-existent with God. God himself, finding he was in the midst of spirits and glory, because he was more intelligent, saw proper to institute laws whereby the rest could have a privilege to advance like himself. The relationship we have with God places us in a situation to advance in knowledge. He has power to institute laws to instruct the weaker intelligences, that they may be exalted with himself, so that they might have one glory upon another, and all that knowledge, power, glory, and intelligence, which is requisite in order to save them in the world of spirits.[3]

Noting what the Prophet said, God did not set up laws and requirements to make us miserable or to curtail our freedoms. On the contrary, those laws and directives were calculated to exalt us. Through untold years of celestial time, we learned by exercising our agency that God's plan for us really was the way to happiness.

After we had progressed as far as possible in our quest to become like Heavenly Father, it was necessary for us to come to earth and take upon ourselves a body and learn to live by faith that which we had learned while in the presence of God. Although earth life was designed to be the final page in our test, it was not designed to be unduly distasteful. We knew we would have problems and challenges, but we readily accepted those challenges because of the vision of what the end result would be. President Joseph F. Smith believed and taught that we knew our lives, our future problems, and our missions before we ever came to this earth.

> Had we not known before we came the necessity of our coming, the importance of obtaining tabernacles, the glory to be achieved in posterity, the grand object to be attained by being tried and tested—weighed in the balance, in the exercise of the divine attributes, god-like powers and free agency with which we are endowed; whereby, after descending below all things, Christ-like, we might ascend above all things, and become like our Father, Mother and Elder Brother, Almighty and Eternal!—we never would have come; that is, if we could have stayed away.
>
> I believe that our Savior is the ever-living example to all flesh in all these things. He no doubt possessed a foreknowledge of all the vicissitudes through which he would have to pass in the mortal tabernacle, when the foundations of this earth were laid, "when the morning stars sang together, and all the sons of God shouted for joy." When he conversed with the brother of Jared, on the Mount, in his spiritual body, he understood his mission, and knew the work he had to do, as thoroughly as when he ascended from the Mount of Olives before the wondering gaze of the Jewish disciples, with his resurrected, glorious and immortal body.
>
> And yet, to accomplish the ultimatum of his previous existence, and consummate the grand and glorious object of his being, and the salvation of his infinite brotherhood, he had to come and take upon him flesh. He is our example. The works he did, we are commanded to do. We are enjoined to follow him, as he followed his Head; that where he is, we may be also; and being with him, may be like him. **If Christ knew beforehand, so did we**. But in coming here, we forgot all, that our agency might be free indeed, to choose good or evil, that we might merit the reward of our own choice and conduct. But by the power of the Spirit, in the redemption of Christ, through obedience, we often catch

> a spark from the awakened memories of the immortal soul, which lights up our whole being as with the glory of our former home.[4]

From our earliest memories on this earth, we have been prompted by the Spirit to be true to our foreordained mission just as the Savior was true to His. Your activity in the Church, your basic desire to keep the commandments, your willingness to humbly submit to the divine requirements of baptism, confirmation, priesthood, endowment, and sealing brought the calm assurance that if you would endure faithfully to the end, you would gain eternal life.

The road of life has not been easy nor smooth. It was intended to be rough and trying. But you have made it this far, and the prospects of you making it successfully to the end loom brighter each day. Through the years of trial and experience, you have learned that the Lord really knew what He was saying when He said, "It is more blessed to give than to receive." The Christ-like joy that comes from service has brought you a wealth of memories that will follow you into eternity. All of the sacrifices of having children, putting your own needs behind those never-ending needs of your family, fulfilling Church assignments, and serving when it was not convenient to serve have all resulted in at least a partial understanding of the Savior's promise, "And if it so be that you should labor all your days in crying repentance unto this people, and bring, save it be one soul unto me, how great shall be your joy with him in the kingdom of my Father!" (D&C 18:15).

With a legacy of sacrifice you are leaving for your children, have you considered the icing on the cake by demonstrating your willingness to subject your will to the will of the Father by responding one more time to His call to serve? If the Father did not know that this mission for the two of you during these golden years was in your best interest eternally, He would not have inspired the living prophets to extend the invitation. All of the questions you may have about your ability, knowledge, skills, language, and so on are really secondary to your willingness to submit your papers and volunteer for the call.

Do the Church leaders realize that many of you are bone tired? Of course. We, too, although still somewhat younger, have experienced the desire to stop for a rest. However, the word of the Lord comes forcefully to mind: "And any man that shall go and preach this gospel of the kingdom, and fail not to continue faithful in all things, shall not be weary in mind, neither darkened, neither in body, limb, nor joint; and a hair of his head shall not fall to the ground unnoticed. And they shall not go hungry, neither athirst" (D&C 84:80).

We have been the recipients of the promised blessings. We have witnessed many senior couples receive the same. We are being led by men who are years past the time when we will be serving missions. What better way of concluding a wonderful, difficult, rewarding mortal life than to conclude your service by giving your all.

> We are all enlisted till the conflict is o'er. Happy are we. Happy are we. Soldiers in the army there's a bright crown in store. We will win and wear it by and by. Haste to the battle, quick to the field; . . .
>
> Hark! The sound of battle sounding loudly and clear; Come join the ranks! Come join the rank! We are waiting now for soldiers; who'll volunteer? . . .
>
> Fighting for a kingdom, and the world is our foe; Happy are we! Happy are we! Glad to join the army, we will sing as we go; We shall gain the vic-t'ry by and by. Dangers may gather—why should we fear? Jesus, our Leader, ever is near. He will protect us, comfort, and cheer. We're joyfully, joyfully marching to our home.
>
> We are all enlisted till the conflict is o'er; Happy are we! (*Hymns*, no. 250).

So, here in the golden part of your lives, still sweethearts after all these years, is there something else for the two of you to do? Are you truly SWEETHEARTS WITH A MISSION?

NOTES

1. Note by Elder B. H. Roberts, *Teachings of the Prophet Joseph Smith*, Notes, 355.
2. *Teachings of the Prophet Joseph Smith*, 354.
3. *Journal of Discourses*, 5–6:7.
4. *Contributor*, 1883, Vol. 4, 114–15 (Joseph Fielding Smith, *Gospel Doctrine*, 13).

APPENDIX

Couples might get on their knees and ask Heavenly Father if the time is right for them to serve a mission together. Of all the qualifications, a desire to serve may be the most important.

—President Russell M. Nelson, "Senior Missionary Moments," *Ensign*, April 2016

Senior missionaries are absolutely critical to our work, We have thousands of them serving. But we only have about half of what we need.

—Elder **Brent H. Nielson**, General Authority Seventy and Executive Director of the Church's Missionary Department.

We're not saying that couples [or individuals] can pick and choose their own missionary assignments, a call is still a call. . . . [But] we talk to our senior couples about their service preferences, and every consideration is given to letting them serve where and how they want to serve.

—Elder Jeffrey R. Holland, "Senior Missionaries: Needed, Blessed, and Loved," *Ensign*, April 2016

Those calls are made possible by the great love of the Savior that His servants know where these wonderful young men and women, senior missionaries, and senior couple missionaries are to serve.

—Elder Ronald A. Rasband, "The Divine Call of a Missionary," April 2010 general conference

When we think of missionaries, we generally picture in our minds young men with shirts and ties and young women dressed modestly. But along with them are marvelous senior missionaries who have answered the pleadings of prophets and apostles for more missionary couples. I express gratitude for our senior missionaries. They are young in spirit, wise, and willing to work.

—President Russell M. Nelson, "Senior Missionaries and the Gospel," October 2004 general conference

In addition to the need for more young men and women to serve, there is an **urgent need for couples.** *Each time we visit a mission, the universal request is for more couples. The need is great for mature couples who are financially able, possessing strong testimonies and with reasonably good health. Their entry into the mission field adds strength and maturity to our missionary effort.*

With the opportunities to labor so plentiful, we need experienced couples to work with those newly converted to the gospel, making sure that the seeds which have fallen on good ground will be nourished and cultivated in order that the tares of a previous life-style will not spring up and choke out the good plants. You mature couples have years of experience in studying, teaching, and administering in the wards and branches of the Church. That experience is so desperately needed throughout the world to prevent the tender new plants from being overcome by worldliness.

You are the ones who can build a firm root structure, which will support the new converts in the truths of the gospel in this life and help them become worthy to receive the blessings in the eternities to come. Listen to the experiences of those couples who have gone forth to serve.

—Elder L. Tom Perry, "But the Labourers Are Few," April 1992 general conference

Having been deeply involved in missionary work for the past several years, I see such glorious opportunities for older couples to continue to be useful in serving their fellowmen. How badly the Church needs us!

There are so many of you who have found fulfillment in serving missions, forgetting yourselves in that important work, staying youthful in the discipline and single-mindedness that come with being immersed in the gospel and sharing your testimonies with all those you meet. I hope I can do the same!

I think of Royce Flandro and his wife, who after retirement served a mission in Spain, performing valuable service. Upon returning home, they missed that beautiful experience, so they came to the Missionary Department to ask where they could help the most. It was suggested to them that they might learn Hungarian, which they did. A few months later they were called to Hungary, once again serving with distinction. Now they are headed for Mongolia.

So many of us are afraid to leave our "comfort zones" and thus cheat ourselves of some of the greatest adventures of our lives. (Read or listen to his whole talk—it is inspiring!)

—Elder Robert Backman, "The Golden Years,"
October 1992 general conference

We are grateful for the thousands who have answered the call to serve, and we are grateful for the valiant missionaries who are going out each week to join in the great harvest that the Lord is hastening. We recognize and appreciate the sacrifice and service of your sons and daughters and the marvelous work being accomplished by them. We appreciate the mature, seasoned couples who leave the comforts of their homes and their beloved children and grandchildren. Your efforts and sacrifices will be a blessing to you, of course.

—Elder David B. Haight, "Missionary Work,"
October 1993 general conference

ABOUT THE AUTHOR

Randy Bott is married to the love of his life, Vickie (fifty years and counting). They have six children, sixteen grandchildren, and one great-granddaughter.

Brother Bott has degrees from Utah State University (a bachelor's in psychology and a master's in secondary education) and a doctorate degree in educational leadership from Brigham Young University. He has served as a bishop, in two stake presidencies, and as a mission president. He served his first mission in Samoa.

After he retired from BYU in 2012, he and his wife served missions at BYU–Hawaii and in Sydney, Australia. They are currently preparing for another mission.

Brother Bott taught in the Church Education System in Utah and North Carolina for twenty years, and nineteen years at BYU–Provo. He has authored many books and articles. His passion is teaching and counseling. He loves people and loves problem-solving and creating new programs to help people succeed.